"In my research in the US and around the world, I have seen how teachers appreciate the collaborative learning offered by lesson study – and how their students benefit from their teachers' growing expertise. This wonderful new book – *Stepping Up Lesson Study: An Educator's Guide to Deeper Learning* – will extend those benefits. Combining the knowledge of lesson study experts across the globe with a wealth of resources and information, the book is filled with practical examples and guidance that will help teachers and teacher educators deepen their understanding of lesson study. I highly recommend this book to all who want to strengthen teaching practices and student learning."

**Linda Darling-Hammond**, *Charles E. Ducommun Professor of Teaching and Teacher Education at Stanford University, USA, and Founding President of the Learning Policy Institute*

"It's easy to get started with Lesson Study, but then what? There are riches to be mined beyond those first steps. *Stepping Up Lesson Study: An Educator's Guide to Deeper Learning* offers insights into how a professional learning community can move to the next level. That's essential, because the more deeply you know about Lesson Study, the more you can grow as a teacher."

**Alan Schoenfeld**, *Elizabeth and Edward Conner Professor of Education at University of California, Berkeley, USA*

"Lesson study has the power to transform teaching by focusing teachers' attention on the teaching-learning process. It provides a clear structure for teachers to engage in a careful, critical examination of the impact of their teaching decisions on student learning. This collection builds on other lesson study guides by providing the next level of support for teachers who want to *go deeper* into their inquiry work. These chapters make visible the very particular aspects of Lesson Study that facilitators and teachers need focus on to strengthen the potential of this form of professional learning to improve classroom teaching. It is this level of detail that is so often missing – but so sorely needed – for professional development to make an impact."

**Elizabeth van Es**, *Professor, University of California, Irvine, USA*

"It has been 20 years since Japanese lesson study has been introduced to the rest of the world which has subsequently developed independently in a variety of contexts. This book explores numerous ways lesson study has extended beyond the shores of Japan, causing it to blossom through collaborative networks of researchers and practitioners. The book contributors work at the forefront of lesson study and explore the most recent developments as they adapted and contextualized lesson study in their respective countries. They bring a wealth of knowledge on the initiatives teachers take to transform their lessons to ensure high-quality learning experiences for all children. This book serves as an excellent guide for lesson study that shows us the way forward by illuminating the future of education in a post-COVID-19 world."

**Kiyomi Akita**, *Dean of Graduate School of Education, The University of Tokyo, Japan*

# Stepping up Lesson Study

This is a much-needed book for educators who want to learn more than just the surface features of lesson study, to deepen the process and learning. Bringing together current knowledge and resources from lesson study practitioners and researchers all over the world, this book provides models and examples of how teachers can learn more deeply and how to support them to learn more in lesson study. The chapters connect current research/educational theories to classroom practices and are filled with examples to illustrate how deeper learning looks with lesson study; for example, highlighting the research process, paying attention to educative talk, using case pupils (students) as the teachers' focus, doing *kyouzai kenkyuu* well, facilitating mock-up lessons and so forth. This is not a basic "how-to" handbook of lesson study, and readers can choose chapters with topics of interest to learn and use the new ideas promptly in their work. Coming from the global network of lesson study educators, the book not only provides new learning guides but also provides stories of how lesson study has been adopted in different cultures and educational contexts.

**Aki Murata** is an independent lesson study researcher in the United States.

**Christine Kim-Eng Lee** is an associate professor in curriculum and teaching at the National Institute of Education, Nanyang Technological University, Singapore.

**WALS-Routledge Lesson Study Series**
Series editors: Christine Kim-Eng Lee, Catherine Lewis,
Kiyomi Akita and Keith Wood

This series aims to provide opportunities for researchers and practitioners in Lesson Study to share their work beyond the boundaries of their countries to an international audience. Lesson Study is increasingly popular as a tool for improving the quality of education and schools around the world. As many countries are adapting and contextualizing Japanese Lesson Study to their own needs in response to educational and curriculum reforms cognizant that what matters most is what happens in classrooms and its impact on teachers and students. As Lesson Study originates from Japan, there is also a need for English Language readers around the world to understand more deeply the underlying philosophies, policies and practices of Japanese Lesson Study in the cultural contexts of their schools and classrooms. As well as original works in English from leading figures in Lesson Study, this series will also make available outstanding Lesson Study publications originally written in Japanese but extended and revised for an English audience.

**Changing Teaching, Changing Teachers**
21st Century Teaching and Learning Through Lesson and Learning Study
*Keith Wood and Saratha Sithamparam*

**Stepping up Lesson Study**
An Educator's Guide to Deeper Learning
*Edited by Aki Murata and Christine Kim-Eng Lee*

# Stepping up Lesson Study
An Educator's Guide to Deeper Learning

Edited by Aki Murata and
Christine Kim-Eng Lee

LONDON AND NEW YORK

First published 2021
by Routledge
2 Park Square, Milton Park, Abingdon, Oxon OX14 4RN

and by Routledge
52 Vanderbilt Avenue, New York, NY 10017

*Routledge is an imprint of the Taylor & Francis Group, an informa business*

© 2021 selection and editorial matter, Aki Murata and Christine Kim-Eng Lee; individual chapters, the contributors

The right of Aki Murata and Christine Kim-Eng Lee to be identified as the authors of the editorial material, and of the authors for their individual chapters, has been asserted in accordance with sections 77 and 78 of the Copyright, Designs and Patents Act 1988.

All rights reserved. No part of this book may be reprinted or reproduced or utilised in any form or by any electronic, mechanical, or other means, now known or hereafter invented, including photocopying and recording, or in any information storage or retrieval system, without permission in writing from the publishers.

*Trademark notice*: Product or corporate names may be trademarks or registered trademarks, and are used only for identification and explanation without intent to infringe.

*British Library Cataloguing-in-Publication Data*
A catalogue record for this book is available from the British Library

*Library of Congress Cataloging-in-Publication Data*
Names: Murata, Aki, editor. | Lee, Christine Kim-eng, editor.
Title: Stepping up lesson study : an educator's guide to deeper learning / edited by Aki Murata and Christine Kim-Eng Lee.
Description: Abingdon, Oxon ; New York, NY : Routledge, 2021. | Includes bibliographical references and index.
Identifiers: LCCN 2020031240 (print) | LCCN 2020031241 (ebook) | ISBN 9780367433390 (hardback) | ISBN 9780367433383 (paperback) | ISBN 9781003002536 (ebook)
Subjects: LCSH: Lesson planning—Study and teaching. | Teachers—In-service training. | Group work in education. | Teaching—Methodology. | Effective teaching.
Classification: LCC LB1027.4 .S74 2021 (print) | LCC LB1027.4 (ebook) | DDC 371.3028—dc23
LC record available at https://lccn.loc.gov/2020031240
LC ebook record available at https://lccn.loc.gov/2020031241

ISBN: 978-0-367-43338-3 (hbk)
ISBN: 978-0-367-43339-0 (pbk)
ISBN: 978-1-003-00253-6 (ebk)

Typeset in Times New Roman
by Apex CoVantage, LLC

# Contents

| | |
|---|---|
| *List of figures* | ix |
| *List of tables* | xi |
| *Contributors* | xii |
| *Foreword* | xvii |
| *Preface* | xix |

1 Introduction   1
AKI MURATA AND CHRISTINE KIM-ENG LEE

2 Lesson study as research: relating lesson goals, activities and data collection   4
AKI MURATA

3 How case pupils, pupil interviews and sequenced research lessons can strengthen teacher insights in *how* to improve learning for all pupils   14
PETER DUDLEY AND JEAN LANG

4 Teacher learning through seeing students' mistakes during inclusive mathematics lesson study   27
JUDITH FABREGA

5 Going deeper into lesson study through *kyouzai kenkyuu*   39
BAN HENG CHOY AND CHRISTINE KIM-ENG LEE

6 Refining the research lesson's instructional approach during lesson study: mock-up lessons   52
SHELLEY FRIEDKIN

7 Strengthening knowledge development in teachers' conversations in lesson study   66
EDEL KARIN KVAM AND ELAINE MUNTHE

8 Scaffolding student teachers' professional noticing when using lesson study  76
GRO NAESHEIM-BJØRKVIK, NINA HELGEVOLD AND DEBORAH SORTON LARSSEN

9 Facilitators' roles in lesson study: from leading the group to doing with the group  86
STÉPHANE CLIVAZ AND ANNE CLERC-GEORGY

10 Facilitating a lesson study team to adopt an inquiry stance  94
SIEBRICH DE VRIES AND IRIS UFFEN

11 Learner-centered facilitation in lesson study groups  106
SHANNON MORAGO AND SVEVA GRIGIONI BAUR

12 Conclusion: how do we judge the success of lesson study adaptations?  116
CATHERINE LEWIS

*Index*  121

# Figures

| | | |
|---|---|---|
| 2.1 | Examples of the rectangles | 5 |
| 2.2 | Problem representation | 5 |
| 2.3 | Example of three research points | 7 |
| 2.4 | Case box 1 | 8 |
| 2.5 | Thinking point 1 | 9 |
| 2.6 | Case box 2 | 10 |
| 2.7 | Case box 3 | 11 |
| 2.8 | Lesson plan format | 11 |
| 2.9 | Case box 4 | 12 |
| 2.10 | Thinking point 2 | 12 |
| 3.1 | Thinking point 1 | 14 |
| 3.2 | School A: post research lesson 2 discussion | 14 |
| 3.3 | School B: post research lesson 3 discussion | 15 |
| 3.4 | School C: post research lesson 3 discussion | 15 |
| 3.5 | School B: post research lesson 3 discussion | 16 |
| 3.6 | Stages in the lesson study process emphasizing the role of case pupils | 17 |
| 3.7 | Thinking point 2 | 18 |
| 3.8 | Thinking point 3 | 18 |
| 3.9 | Example 1 | 19 |
| 3.10 | Example 2 | 19 |
| 3.11 | Example 3 | 20 |
| 3.12 | Example 4 | 21 |
| 3.13 | Thinking point 4 | 22 |
| 3.14 | Example 5 | 22 |
| 3.15 | Example 6 | 22 |
| 4.1 | Examples of manipulatives uses for $16 - 12$ (e.g. "There are 16 red flowers and 12 white flowers. How many more red flowers are there?") | 30 |
| 4.2 | Thinking box 1: open-ended lesson activity | 30 |
| 4.3 | Thinking box 2: how students think through mistakes | 33 |
| 4.4 | Thinking box 3: the relationship between open-ended activity, multiple student solutions and learning from making mistakes | 35 |
| 5.1 | A possible student error of calculating "run" | 47 |
| 5.2 | Different types of questions in the worksheet | 47 |
| 6.1 | The mock-up lesson as part of the lesson study process | 52 |
| 6.2 | Anticipated student responses | 54 |
| 6.3 | Board plan after the mock-up lesson | 55 |

| | | |
|---|---|---|
| 6.4 | Initial version of the board plan based on student type B's anticipated response | 56 |
| 6.5 | Board plan for student type A responses | 56 |
| 6.6 | Progression of three student responses | 57 |
| 6.7 | Excerpt from the team's research lesson plan, page 3 | 59 |
| 6.8 | Lesson problem | 60 |
| 6.9 | Partial board plan during the mock-up | 61 |
| 6.10 | Board plan after the mock-up lesson | 63 |
| 6.11 | Excerpt from district-published *Elementary School Guide to Examining Content and Unit Planning* document | 64 |
| 7.1 | Identify relevant perspectives needed to address the task at hand | 72 |
| 10.1 | Characteristics of an inquiry stance | 94 |
| 10.2 | Characteristics of exploratory talk versus cumulative talk | 95 |
| 10.3 | Connecting theory and practice | 96 |
| 10.4 | Individual utterances that show lack of exploration | 96 |
| 10.5 | Helpful questions in preparation for the group protocol | 98 |
| 10.6 | Basic ground rules of exploratory conversations | 98 |
| 10.7 | Helpful questions for discussing the communication in the lesson study team | 99 |
| 10.8 | Summarized suggestions for a facilitator to support teachers to adopt an inquiry stance by creating a safe climate | 99 |
| 10.9 | A goal system interview | 101 |
| 10.10 | Ingredients for the research question | 102 |
| 10.11 | Critical reflective dialogue | 102 |
| 10.12 | Stimulating depth by modelling exploratory talk | 103 |
| 10.13 | Themes for reflection and consolidation | 104 |
| 10.14 | Summarized suggestions for a facilitator to support teachers to adopt an inquiry stance by guiding participants through the process | 105 |
| 11.1 | What learner-centered facilitation is and isn't | 107 |
| 11.2 | LS group norms | 108 |
| 11.3 | LS process guidelines | 109 |
| 11.4 | LS facilitator guidelines | 110 |
| 12.1 | Visible features and underlying changes of lesson study | 117 |
| 12.2 | Mathematics SBAC, John Muir Elementary School (San Francisco) | 119 |

# Tables

| | | |
|---|---|---|
| 3.1 | Post lesson discussion record RL1 (the LS group's agreed notes) | 23 |
| 4.1 | Teacher demographic data; all names are pseudonyms | 28 |
| 4.2 | Levels of conception of quantities | 37 |
| 5.1 | Framework of the content of the unit on "light" | 41 |
| 5.2 | Description of the three-point framework | 44 |
| 7.1 | Less developed and more developed forms of lesson study | 74 |
| 8.1 | An example of a completed *kyouzai kenkyuu* record sheet | 79 |
| 11.1 | Themes related to the role of facilitators | 114 |

# Contributors

**Sveva Grigioni Baur** is a natural sciences and biology teacher in secondary schools in Lausanne, Switzerland. She has completed a doctoral thesis in marine biology and experimental microbiology carried out in Paris at the Muséum National d'Histoire Naturelle and a three-year postdoctorate at the University of Geneva. She is also an associate professor in natural sciences and biology didactics in the Research Unit of Mathematics and Natural Science at the HEP Vaud, Switzerland, since 2007, and a member of the board of the Lausanne Lesson Study Laboratory (3LS) since 2013. Practicing lesson studies as a facilitator for ten years, she developed with Dr Shannon Morago the "learner-centred facilitation" approach for LS international pre-service teachers groups and in-service mathematics and science teachers LS groups. She is currently working in LS international collaborations with Dr Shannon Morago (HSU, California), Dr Chiara Bertonini (UNIMORE, Italy) and Dr John Mynott (University of Aberdeen, Scotland).

**Ban Heng Choy** is an assistant professor (mathematics education) at the Mathematics and Mathematics Education Academic Group, National Institute of Education, Nanyang Technological University, Singapore. Specializing in mathematics teacher noticing, his work has focused on developing mathematics teachers' ability to notice important instructional details so that they are able to learn from their own teaching. His research interests include task design, orchestrating discussions and assessment in mathematics education. His current research projects are centred on mathematics teacher professional learning, lesson study, mathematics teacher education and STEM education.

**Anne Clerc-Georgy** is a professor at the Lausanne University of Teacher Education (HEP Vaud), Switzerland. She is in charge of the teaching and research unit "Teaching, Learning and Evaluation". She is co-founder of the Lausanne Laboratory Lesson Study (3LS). Her work focuses on the role of knowledge and education in learning and development and is part of the fight against the creation of inequalities in education. She is interested in the process of training students in teaching and learning in the early years of schooling. More particularly, through lesson studies, she contributes to the development of a play-based didactic aiming at the fundamental learning of schooling.

**Stéphane Clivaz** is a professor of mathematics education at Lausanne University of Teacher Education (HEP Vaud), Switzerland. After completing his MA in mathematics, he was a secondary math teacher and a head of department for more than ten years. He completed his PhD in 2011 (University of Geneva). In 2014 he published a book about the influence of teachers' mathematical knowledge on their teaching in primary school. In 2018, he also co-authored a mathematics book for primary teachers. He was co-founder in 2014 of the

Lausanne Laboratory Lesson Study (3LS). He is also an executive committee member of the World Association of Lesson Studies (WALS).

**Peter Dudley** is an education leader, writer and researcher. He has taught primary and secondary education in London and abroad and held education leadership posts nationally and internationally. He directed the UK government's Primary National Strategy from 2006 to 2011 and pioneered the development of "networked learning community" school systems including London's "Camden Learning" as director of education from 2013 to 2019. He introduced Lesson Study into the UK from Japan in 2001, leading its UK development through Research Lesson Study (RLS). His research on teacher learning in RLS was shortlisted for BERA's 2013 Doctoral Research award. His RLS handbook was published in 2005, and his book *Lesson Study: Professional Learning for Our Time* was published in 2015. He now lectures in educational leadership and learning at the University of Cambridge. He develops and researches collaborative educational improvement in classrooms, schools and systems. He became president of WALS in 2016 and is active in Oracy Cambridge and Hughes Hall's Research-Practice Bridge.

**Judith Fabrega** is the co-founder of Kabana, an educational centre for families and educators. She earned her master's degree in development in mathematics and science at the University of California, Berkeley, and her doctorate in curriculum and instruction at the University of Florida. Judith has been a preschool and kindergarten teacher and has worked with many elementary schools in the United States and Spain. Her main interest is investigating teacher and student learning through planning and implementing lessons. She is also interested in developing tools to further help teachers to improve how they understand student thinking and consequently improve *all* student achievement. In her work at Kabana, she is producing professional development for in-service teachers.

**Shelley Friedkin** is a senior research associate for lesson study group at Mills College in Oakland, California. She graduated from Brunel University in England with an elementary teaching credential and taught in Central London. She received her doctorate in education leadership from Mills College. For over fifteen years she has collaborated on the design, implementation and management of US school site and district studies to develop teacher learning and lesson study. These include the program development and testing of Japanese Teaching Through Problem-Solving (TTP) and the implementation and testing of research-based toolkits to improve lesson study. More recently she has been developing resources to support and grow school-wide lesson study.

**Nina Helgevold** is working with and doing research related to lesson study as professional development for pre-service and in-service teachers as a professor at University of Stavanger, Norway (UiS). This involves collaborations with schools and school owners. She was involved in a Norwegian research funded project on Lesson Study in Initial Teacher Education (2012–2015). She is currently involved in a lesson study project in Malawi for primary teachers in mathematics. Besides several published research articles on lesson study, she has written a book with two colleagues at UiS on lesson study in Norway (2015) and co-edited a recent anthology, *Lesson Study in Initial Teacher Education* (Emerald, 2018). She is a council member of the World Association of Lesson Studies (WALS).

**Edel Karin Kvam** is an associate professor of education in the Department of Education at Faculty of Psychology, University of Bergen, Norway. She was first a teacher in primary school in Norway and has been a teacher educator for many years. Her research interests are teacher professional development, teacher collaboration and mentoring of students, new teachers and colleagues.

**Jean Lang** is currently a research student at the University of Exeter following a 44-year career as a teacher, head teacher and local and national education leader. Her interest in lesson study began when she introduced it to 100 schools in a large district as part of a national project in 2007. As a senior officer in a London borough, she jointly led a project to introduce the new mathematics curriculum using lesson study. This project spread to ninety schools across London and was sustained through local hubs. She has worked with Pete Dudley on developing the website "Lesson Study UK", helping to create resources which are freely available to help schools introduce and sustain lesson study. She is the current Honorary General Secretary of the World Association of Lesson Studies (WALS) and is carrying out worldwide research focusing on the factors that seem to make LS sustainable.

**Deborah Sorton Larssen** is an associate professor at the University of Stavanger in Norway and teaches and researches at the Institute of Teacher Education. She works primarily with student teachers who are studying to become English as a foreign language teachers in Norwegian schools. Introducing and embedding lesson study in a sustainable way with her students, both at the BA and MA levels, has offered a rich field for experience and research into working with lesson study with relatively inexperienced student teachers. How lesson study can be adapted so that it is meaningful and purposeful both for the student teachers and their mentors has been an important focus for her work. Her work in lesson study within teacher education has also led to a productive network collaboration with colleagues from the Universities of Leicester and Valencia.

**Christine Kim-Eng Lee** is an associate professor of policy, Curriculum and Leadership Academic Group, National Institute of Education (NIE), Nanyang Technological University (NTU), Singapore. She is currently the Programme Director of NIE's joint MA in Leadership and Educational Change with Teachers College, Columbia University, New York. She held several leadership positions as academic group head and vice dean at NIE over sixteen years. Lesson study is widespread in both mainstream and special education schools in Singapore through her pioneering and tireless efforts. She played an active role in the international lesson study community as president of the World Association of Lesson Studies (WALS) from 2011 to 2016 and is now its immediate past president. She is a recipient of the Teachers College Distinguished Alumni Award and NTU's Nanyang Award for Excellent Service. Her research interests are in the areas of curriculum reforms, teacher learning, lesson study, collaborative learning and listening pedagogy.

**Catherine Lewis** is a research scientist at Mills College, Oakland, California. She earned her doctorate in developmental psychology at Stanford with a minor in Japanese studies, and she has worked to make Japanese elementary education practices and materials available to US educators with a particular focus on lesson study (teacher-led, classroom-based professional learning) and mathematics Teaching Through Problem-Solving (an approach in which students build each new mathematical idea in the curriculum). She has directed ten major grants funded by NSF, IES, or private foundations focused on instructional improvement, including a randomized trial of teacher-led lesson study with Japanese mathematical resources (Lewis & Perry, *JRME*, 2017, 48:3) that was identified by a *What Works Clearinghouse* criteria review as one of only two studies of mathematics professional learning (of 643 reviewed) to improve students' mathematical proficiency. Her recent work demonstrates the potential of school-wide lesson study to dramatically improve achievement in urban settings.

**Shannon Morago** has been an instructor and programme leader at the Humboldt State University School of Education since 2005 and a high school science and math teacher at Six Rivers Charter High School/NOHUM since 1996. She received the Carlston Outstanding Teacher of America award in 2011 and earned her doctorate from the University of California, Davis, in 2015, studying how pre-service teachers in LS groups learn to teach diverse students. She is a member of Lausanne Laboratory of Lesson Study (3LS) at the Haute Ecole Pédagogique de Lausanne (HEP Vaud), Switzerland, and has collaborated with Dr Sveva Grigioni Baur since 2009, co-developing a learner-centred facilitation approach while leading eight international pre-service STEM LS groups.

**Elaine Munthe** is a professor of education and the Director of the Knowledge Center for Education at the University of Stavanger, Norway. She is a pioneer of lesson study in Norway, working with the very first schools that established lesson study as their approach to professional learning and school development. Her research interests are qualifying for teaching, teachers' work and learning and systematic reviews.

**Aki Murata** is an independent educational researcher, writer, speaker and activist. Having served as a professor of education at Stanford University and University of California, Berkeley, she continues to work with educators at different career levels, in various roles and in multiple dimensions, to improve teaching and learning for increased opportunities for students who are otherwise marginalized. Her work has appeared in many influential journals, books, and other media, and she is globally considered as one of the key lesson study practitioners.

**Gro Naesheim-Bjørkvik** is an associate professor at the University of Stavanger in Norway, where she teaches various courses related to physical education in teacher education at the bachelor's and master's levels. Her research focus is on teacher education, mentoring and professional development through lesson study. Working with lesson study within teacher education has also led to a productive network collaboration with colleagues from the Universities of Leicester and Valencia. Together they have solved many of the challenges of adapting lesson study to the practicum arena.

**Iris Uffen** is a PhD candidate in the Teacher Education Department of the University of Groningen. Her research project is one of the research grants that the consortium Lesson Study NL has acquired. Her research focuses on in-depth insight of teachers' learning processes during lesson study and how facilitators can contribute in optimizing these learning processes. She is particularly interested in the benefits for learning of different kinds of "teacher talk". She is also involved in lesson study facilitators training and in the guidance and assessment of student teachers performing lesson study in the context of their teacher training.

**Siebrich de Vries** came across lesson study during her PhD trajectory in the field of teacher learning and student orientation. In 2013 she introduced lesson study in the north of the Netherlands through the organization of two lesson study PLCs, a collaboration of twelve secondary schools and two teacher training institutes. At that time, she also introduced lesson study in teacher training. In 2016, she founded the consortium Lesson Study NL together with Sui Lin Goei and Nellie Verhoef. Together they wrote a practical manual for lesson study in Dutch educational practice and developed a website (https://lessonstudynl.nl/); they also organize annual lesson study conferences and apply for funding for research. She currently works as a professor of Vital Subject Pedagogy at NHL Stenden University of Applied Sciences and as an assistant professor in the Teacher Education Department at the University of Groningen, where she supervises several PhD candidates in the field of lesson study.

# Foreword

In just a little over two decades, lesson study has gone from a little-known Asian practice to a well-known innovation embraced by educators in many regions of the world. The annual conference of the World Association of Lesson Studies regularly attracts capacity crowds and has been held in countries ranging from Brunei, Thailand, Japan, Singapore, Hong Kong and China in Asia to the United Kingdom, Sweden and the Netherlands in Europe. This volume alone represents work conducted in the Netherlands, Norway, Singapore, Switzerland, the United Kingdom and the United States. Why is there so much interest in lesson study?

Teachers have the very challenging job of transforming scientific and pedagogical knowledge into practice. Teachers need a learning system that allows them not only to keep building knowledge but also to enact it in practice. Ideally their learning system needs to be collegial, so that teachers can learn from one another's experiences and can build coherent instruction across classrooms and grade levels throughout a school. The learning system needs to involve cycles of experimentation, since finding out how planned instruction actually unfolds in the classroom is how much teacher learning takes place. Lesson study is such a system: collaborative, practice-based cycles that allow teachers to study cutting-edge research and use it to inform their classroom practice, working with colleagues to design and study instruction.

This volume provides accounts of how teachers in a variety of countries have adapted lesson study to their local settings. We learn about the power of identifying focal students to be studied, predicting each student's response to the planned instruction and then carefully observing and document students' actual responses. Japanese educators often say that lesson study gives teachers "the eyes to see students," and observation of focal students provides a powerful way to build such vision. We also learn about the power of conducting *kyouzai kenkyuu* – study of curriculum materials, including both the textbook itself and additional resources that illuminate the underlying content and what is known about its teaching and learning. We learn about the power of open-ended mathematics tasks to spark teachers' appreciation of the value of examining student mistakes.

Many readers will learn for the first time about "mock-up lessons," which are not widely known outside Japan. With colleagues playing the role of "students," the mock-up lesson allows the instructor to test out crucial segments of the lesson – for example, the specific questions to pose about each student solution strategy and the visual and written information to be recorded on the board. Mock-up lessons help the lesson study team imagine how the lesson will play out in the "swiftly flowing river" of classroom life and can provide a powerful way to bridge the gap from knowing to doing.

Improving teaching requires integration of knowledge from formal resources and from team members' own experiences, and several chapters provide frameworks and tools to support group processes, facilitation and a research mindset that will enable ongoing learning from one another and from practice.

This volume is diverse not only in the geographical location of the work but also in the lesson study participants (e.g. pre-service and in-service) and content areas under study (mathematics, science, physical education, language). My deepest thanks to the volume editors, Aki Murata and Christine Kim-Eng Lee, for their tireless effort in bringing this work to fruition, and to all the authors for bringing their work to the public.

*Catherine Lewis*
*Distinguished Research Scientist*
*Mills College, United States*
*WALS-Routledge Lesson Study Series Editorial Board*

# Preface

As this volume nears its completion, I am socially isolated in my small apartment in Chicago in the middle of the COVID-19 pandemic. It feels surreal that the book is finally coming together now, since this project has been on my calendar since late 2016. It was an idea my friend, Elaine Munthe, and I exchanged over emails: "Wouldn't it be nice to have a book for teachers who want to do more than simply following basic procedures of lesson study?" I recall how the idea made sense to me, and we quickly put together a book proposal. Four years after the conversation, the book is finally coming out this year.

As many of you already know, it is not typical for a book to take four years to publish, even when it requires coordinating the work of multiple chapter authors, like this volume. There was indeed a very long and unusual break between book proposal submission and approval. Seeing other lesson study books being published during that time, I assumed my ideas had been forgotten in the vast universe (and I am glad they weren't).

With the pandemic, many of us now had to reconceptualize what time and space mean in our lives. With everything being suddenly paused, many became more thoughtful and purposeful, taking time to re-evaluate and reprioritize things we do. However, this happens quite a lot in my professional life (with or without a pandemic). While I tend to move quickly and finish my work early, the work around me often does not sync with my rhythm and loses its momentum, and now I wonder if that has something to do with my professional trajectory so far. In the past years, I switched institutions a few times and ended up leaving academia. It was a painful period, and I am still trying to make sense of the significance of this book being published now, when I no longer belong to the so-called ivory tower. Most contributors to this book belong to the world of academia, and I am an odd one out. I never cared about affiliations, ranks or status, and it feels good to be purely myself as this book comes out in print.

As the Black Lives Matter movement and its messages are ubiquitous in this historical time, I remain hopeful that we may see lasting changes. My time in academia was filled with promises that did not come true and opportunities that were not available to me. Many well-intentioned colleagues explained how it had nothing to do with the quality of my scholarship but everything to do with who I was (my cultural ways, my background, my connections), and I should not take it personally that I was not receiving the promised recognitions as others, as there was very little I could do about it. Like me, there are thousands of students who attend schools while their home cultures are not reflected in their school experiences. They can be quickly dismissed by their teachers, as their different ways of thinking and learning are not something the teachers know to pay attention to. Lesson study, when used in purposeful ways, can guide teachers to pause, listen, examine meanings of what students are saying, and understand why. Reflective and committed teachers will then use the new understanding to improve their instruction, thus keep learning about their students. I have witnessed many beautiful moments in lesson study like that, and these are golden nuggets of my memories.

What has always been a constant in my work is my commitment to the students who come from different communities and the teachers who teach them. I have created lifelong connections with these teachers, and it has given me much happiness knowing how my ideas lived in their teaching practices. And this volume makes yet another mark in the field for that. So, it all comes back, completing the circle, to me. I hope the readers of this book will use the new information and resources to try to understand their not-so-typical students better through lesson study. When some students (minority students, especially) do not perform as you expect them to, take it up as a focus of lesson study, plan how to examine and understand the phenomenon better, and apply the new learning in your instruction. The ideas in this book will certainly guide the process. I hope that this book will inspire you to think more deeply about students' different learning paths and know how a little extra time you spend will make a significant difference in students' lives who do not otherwise have access to opportunities. Do speak up when others attribute student surface performance to something they cannot control (e.g. race, culture), and find ways to help all students in your classrooms. I am relying on you.

*Aki Murata, PhD*
*June 2020*
*Chicago, Illinois, USA*

My foray into lesson study began by chance. It was at a cooperative learning conference in Singapore in 2004 when I first heard about lesson study from a group of Japanese academics from University of Tokyo. They brought with them Catherine Lewis as a discussant for their symposium. The idea of lesson study as a collaborative form of teacher professional development and learning that was in situ piqued my interest. Lesson study gives teachers agency in the form and substance of their own inquiries into student learning. Catherine Lewis's apt description of lesson study as "developing your eyes to see children" has stayed with me from the beginning. It seems simple and yet in reality highly complex and not so easy to do as classroom events unfold in rapid succession.

My three-month stint as visiting scholar at the University of Tokyo cemented my passion for lesson study. I had many opportunities to visit schools and observe research lessons with the generous support of Kiyomi Akita, Manabu Sato and Ryoko Tsuneyoshi and their graduate students who served as my translators. I was amazed at the large number of observers at open research lessons and in Hamanogo Elementary School; they were in the hundreds. It was fascinating to observe children up close as they interacted with their teachers, peers, tasks and materials, seemingly oblivious to the many observers clicking away with their video cameras and mobile phones. Listening to teachers and invited critical commentators at open research lesson discussions brought into sharper focus that learning extends beyond that one research lesson, opening a window into a vision of education of how teaching and learning could be.

But seeing how lesson study is conducted in Japanese schools as an observer is not enough. I am a deep believer in "learning by doing" accompanied by reflection. It was in "my doing" with teachers and students in several schools in Singapore through numerous lesson study cycles since 2005 that my conviction deepened about the power of lesson study. Lesson study has the potential to bring about transformational change in teachers as they develop greater understanding of how students learn as they experienced the enacted curriculum. My partnership with schools in Singapore through lesson study has led me to forge long-lasting friendships with many school leaders and teachers. It gives me much joy that my pioneering lesson study work that began in two schools in 2005 with my colleagues from the National Institute of Education, Nanyang Technological University has grown to include about 50% of all schools in Singapore.

Like Aki Murata and Elaine Munthe, I too have sensed the need for teachers to go beyond the surface features of lesson study cycles and deepen their understanding of the myriad ways lesson study "could open their eyes to see children". When the opportunity arose for me to support Aki Murata as a co-editor, I stepped up to support Aki's and Elaine's vision for this book. I hope the ideas contained in this book by our chapter contributors from many parts of the world, many of whom are members of the World Association of Lesson Studies, will give you much to chew on and to experiment in your own journey in lesson study. My own learning is ongoing. It is a privilege for me to work with Aki Murata and all our chapter contributors. They have energized my own understanding of lesson study in nuanced and deeper ways.

*Christine Kim-Eng Lee*
*July 2020*
*Singapore*

# 1 Introduction

*Aki Murata and Christine Kim-Eng Lee*

As lesson study becomes a familiar name for teacher professional development in schools across different countries, we hear an increasing number of inquiries from teachers, lesson study facilitators and teacher educators about how to deepen teacher learning in the process. Lesson study is a teacher professional effort that originated in Japan over 100 years ago, aiming at helping teachers explore students' learning and implement effective teaching practices. Ever since the end of World War II, but especially throughout the 1980s and 1990s, lesson study supported a shift to more student-centred teaching practices among Japanese teachers, and during the last twenty years it has also received global attention outside of Japan. Many educators who have tried lesson study by initially following the four-step procedure in general (goal setting, planning, teaching and debriefing) enjoyed the focused opportunities to consider student learning, with meaningful (practical and locally grounded) professional collaboration they had never experienced before. The opportunities to observe live lessons were particularly meaningful as they develop deeper insights into student learning. As educators attempt to engage in lesson study further, they want to continue to learn more and feel the need for additional guidance to deepen the process. This book came about as a response to these inquiries.

This book consists of the most current knowledge and resources for educators with prior lesson study experience. Each chapter addresses important lesson-study-related topic(s) for which the author(s), through their research and experience of working alongside teachers, have come to develop deeper understanding of the complexities and challenges of doing lesson study. The authors come from around the world and they are each considered lesson study experts, with their own work having pioneered lesson study in their respective countries. As lesson study values usable knowledge in practice, the knowledge in each chapter has also been developed in the author's practice.

Each chapter has rich examples and thinking point boxes, which are designed to challenge the readers to reflect on their own practice and make connections in different lesson study contexts. The authors generously made their resources available to the readers so that the ideas can be adapted and readily used in different lesson study groups. Altogether, the book delivers our cutting-edge work with lesson study in hope of providing the readers with usable ideas.

We start the book with Murata (Chapter 2) describing how to create and maintain the research focus through the lesson study process. Lesson study is teacher research, and the chapter illustrates the process of making connections among lesson goals, activities and data, emphasizing research connections and adding clarity to teachers' learning. In Chapter 3, Dudley and Lang explain how case pupils, pupil interviews and sequenced research lessons help teachers deepen their learning of all pupils' learning. Purposeful examination of a few case pupils' thinking helps create concrete understanding of whole-class learning with reasonable patterns, leading to effective teaching to support student learning based on the patterns. Fabrega (Chapter 4) then presents an example of lesson study where teachers learn about student math thinking by carefully analyzing student mistakes. She emphasizes the importance of open-ended lesson activities that invite different student thinking, making the learning process (including mistakes) visible for the teachers. Together, Chapters 2–4 illustrate the importance of careful research on student learning in lesson study.

Chapters 5–8 are about different angles and tools lesson study groups may use to improve their practice. Choy and Lee (Chapter 5) introduce *kyouzai kenkyuu* as the curriculum study phase in lesson study where teachers examine key teaching and learning materials through the perspectives of students. *Kyouzai kenkyuu* is a daily practice of lesson study in Japan but is often a neglected phase in lesson study adopted in countries beyond Japan. The chapter provides clear description of the process, its purposes and examples of how to support teachers to engage in it. Friedkin (Chapter 6) illustrates how a mock-up lesson taught as a part of the planning phase can reveal student thinking for teachers and help them to refine research lesson plans with increasing understanding of student thinking. Similar to Dudley and Lang's earlier chapter, this chapter describes how lesson study is a process of investigating student learning, where teachers continuously improve teaching through it; the goal is not about teaching the perfect lesson. Kvam and Munthe (Chapter 7) focus on strengthening teachers' talk during lesson study conversations and their outcomes. The chapter provides useful protocols for teachers to engage in exploratory talk and highlights the importance of assessing different knowledge sources, both internal and external, to enhance teachers' own learning possibilities in lesson study. Naesheim-Bjørkvik, Helgevold and Larssen (Chapter 8) focus on the importance of teacher noticing, and how we may guide teachers' attention to notice certain aspects of classroom practices, to invite deeper learning. Using the case of pre-service education, the authors describe the ways to guide teachers' attention, which is applicable beyond pre-service lesson study.

The last three chapters of the book (Chapters 9–11) are about facilitation of lesson study. Developing effective facilitation practices with lesson study is crucial to deepening teacher learning from lesson study and it supports the scaling-up of lesson study within and across educational settings. Clivaz and Clerc-Georgy (Chapter 9) present the evolution of the roles of facilitators over multiple lesson study cycles from convenor, teacher trainer and group member to researcher. Using examples, the authors highlight the key turning points created by facilitators to push teachers from being mere participants in lesson study to co-researchers to help the readers understand and adapt the new facilitator roles. De Vries and Uffen (Chapter 10) address how important it is for teachers to adopt an inquiry stance in their lesson study and the role of the facilitator in supporting teachers to adopt this stance. The authors outline the facilitation of lesson study that help teachers create a new practical knowledge that will no longer be personal and unconscious but joint and explicit, highlighting the importance of exploratory talk, critical reflective dialogue and research in a climate of mutual trust. Morago and Grigioni Baur (Chapter 11) describe learner-centred facilitation and how it helps teachers think and reflect deeply about their student learning and teaching. Using examples of teacher education collaboration across two different countries, the chapter illustrates a unique lesson study context where pre-service teachers collaboratively learned together by becoming aware of their own beliefs and orientations towards certain teaching practices.

You may read the book from beginning to end, which would provide a logical path of deepening lesson study process, starting from reconfirming the importance of student learning and how to research it, to different angles and new practices you may incorporate to deepen lesson study process, and finally to facilitation methods and approaches for increased learning. If you have particular interest in one topic or another, you may start with certain chapters and then follow up with the rest. Each chapter is written in ways to help lesson study educators find and apply usable knowledge in practice, and there is no right or wrong way to take advantage of them and learn. Our suggestion is for you to experiment with the wealth of ideas contained in this book in your search for what will work in your specific contexts.

As the lesson study community grows internationally, it is our sincere hope as the editors of this book that you would find ways to deepen your own learning through lesson study with the practical knowledge presented in this book.

# 2 Lesson study as research
## Relating lesson goals, activities and data collection

*Aki Murata*

As you gain experience with lesson study and move beyond merely following prescribed steps, continuing success of your lesson study depends on many factors, and one important factor to consider is how closely the team can identify the connections among (1) research lesson goals, (2) lesson problem and (3) student learning data collected during the lesson. Lesson study is a research process, and like all other research, logical connections among research questions, research methods and the quality of data collected can make the process meaningful. This makes the discussion you have during lesson debrief focused, resulting in deeper learning. In this chapter, I will outline this challenge by presenting a detailed example first, illustrating how an actual lesson study team experienced the misalignment through the research process despite good intentions, followed by step-by-step guidelines for how to build research within lesson study so that you will gain better insight into student learning.

### An example of a Grade 4 lesson study on area and perimeter (mathematics)

*Before the lesson*

A group of pre-service teachers collaboratively planned a math lesson on measurement, about area and perimeter, for Grade 4 students in an urban district in California. They decided on the content after talking with their mentor teachers about challenging topics to teach for the grade level. Since pre-service teachers had little experience teaching the topic, they conducted an informal interview assessment with a handful of students from four practicum classrooms to understand how students currently thought about the topic. The worksheet included a few items that helped the pre-service teachers assess the following points: (1) Can a student give definitions of area and perimeter? (2) Can a student find the area and perimeter of a rectangle ($4 \times 6$) drawn on grid paper? (3) Can a student give area and perimeter formulas?

After collecting student work, pre-service teachers found that most fourth-grade students could not give precise definitions of area or perimeter (1), and very few students could write the formulas (3). In finding the area and perimeter of a $4 \times 6$ rectangle (2), some students simply added $4 + 6 = 10$ for either perimeter or area, showing they did not understand what perimeter or area was. Higher-performing students who knew about perimeter added each side of the rectangle to find it, and some students who knew about area counted the number of squares in the rectangle. The team concluded that most students did not know what area and perimeter were, thus the research lesson should introduce the concepts by hands-on activities.

They collaboratively decided their lesson goal to be: *Students will understand the concepts of area and perimeter and be able to find the area and perimeter of a rectangle.*

### Planning research lesson

In examining curricular materials and sample lessons, the team found a lesson that asked students to find the largest bulletin board they can create given the length of the border materials. They thought it would be an engaging lesson and very relevant to their classroom lives (bulletin boards). After much deliberations, the teachers decided on the focal lesson problem as follows:

> We have 20 feet of tape-like border materials to frame a bulletin board to display our classroom work. What is the largest area of bulletin board we can create?

### The research lesson

This problem indeed proved to create an engaging lesson. Students were given 1 ft × 1 ft squares and the 20 feet of border materials, to create and examine the area of each bulletin board in small groups. Before starting the activity, the instructor of the lesson also asked students what area and perimeter are and briefly reviewed the concepts.

After the exploration, during the whole-class sharing, students explained how a 5 × 5 square produced the largest area compared to other rectangles they had created. Most groups found the answer by trial and error, rather unsystematically, so seeing all possible rectangles made as a whole class helped the students see certain patterns, and they discussed how surprised they were that the square had the larger area than skinnier/longer rectangles they could create with the border materials (see Figure 2.1).

Next, extending that activity, students completed worksheet problems in small groups, which had various rectangles for students to find areas and perimeters. The lesson study team identified this as a main data collection point, for which they carefully chose different configurations of rectangles. Actual worksheets, the team reasoned, would provide concrete learning data for lesson debrief later on. All observers also took careful notes on student discussions as they filled out the worksheet (see Figure 2.2).

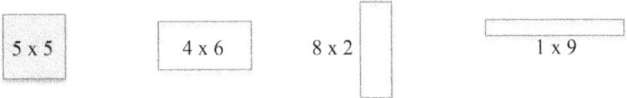

*Figure 2.1* Examples of the rectangles

Find the area and perimeter of the rectangle below:

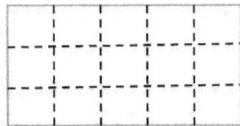

*Figure 2.2* Problem representation

### Lesson debrief

In the lesson debrief, teachers shared their observations of student learning based on the data they had collected. They shared how some students were counting the squares within given rectangles to find the areas, and also counted and added the lengths of the sides to find perimeters. They also observed that some students used formulas, although they were not discussed during the lesson. It appeared that students used the strategies they had known before the lesson to solve the problems on the worksheet. Given the engaging lesson, teachers wondered what happened. Didn't the students learn anything in the lesson?

### Yes, they did learn something

What they learned was not reflected in the data collected (worksheet problems). The important learning in the lesson was how area and perimeter are related. The students learned how different configurations of sides of a rectangle could produce varied areas, and area and perimeter of a shape are interdependent of each other in certain ways. They also learned that visual clues may be misleading in identifying areas, as the very long and skinny rectangle they created ($1 \times 9$) produced a much smaller area compared to the $5 \times 5$ square.

### What could the lesson study team have done differently?

First of all, this lesson could be two lessons, and the teachers may use the first lesson (the bulletin board activity) as the research lesson, as it revealed student thinking. They could possibly have different lesson goals for the two lessons, with the overarching goal being *Students will understand the concepts of area and perimeter*, the goal of the first lesson being *Students will be able to identify relationships and differences between area and perimeter*, and the goal of the second lesson being *Students will be able to find area and perimeter of rectangles*. For the research lesson (Lesson 1), before students experiment with creating different rectangles, the teacher could ask them how they thought area and perimeter are related. If they make different rectangles with the same length around (perimeter), would they all have the same area? Record their hypothesis for later discussion. After the activity, in the whole group discussion, the teacher could ask the students what they now thought the relationships between areas and perimeters are given the shapes they had made (e.g. they are not the same; the same perimeter does not always produce the same area; the skinnier the rectangle is, the smaller the area is). This discussion would be a valuable data collection opportunity. Observers could take notes as the main learning data, students could also write individually (or in small groups) and the team could collect the writings as the data to be discussed later on.

The three research points will look like this (see Figure 2.3).

In this way, the goals of the lesson, lesson activity and data collected by the teachers are all closely related, thus the research process is streamlined and connected, and the lesson debrief discussion would be focused. It is also rewarding for teachers to experience how the lesson made a difference in student thinking of area and perimeter (comparing what they hypothesize at the beginning of the lesson and what they say at the end). The lesson helps students to experience perimeters and areas and to understand the meanings of what they are. This is an important concept development before learning to find area and perimeter in more formal ways (using formulas, etc.).

| Goals of the lesson | Lesson activity | Data collection |
|---|---|---|
| Students will understand the concepts of area and perimeter and be able to identify differences and relationships between area and perimeter. | Finding areas of different rectangles that share same length of perimeter. | After the lesson activity, how do students discuss area and perimeter? Given the different areas they found with rectangles that have same length of perimeter, how do they explain the relationships between them? |

*Figure 2.3* Example of three research points

It should also be noted how the assessment items the pre-service teachers chose (before the lesson and for the lesson) were very prescriptive and likely to have come from their own school experiences as children. In order to have a lesson that reveals student thinking, the lesson must be sufficiently open, using open-ended problems and questions, and thus open-ended assessment. For example, a pre-service teacher could ask students to draw their own rectangles, and ask them to explain where area and perimeters are (open-ended assessment) while taking notes on their explanations. Open-ended problems mean that the problems invite multiple entry points and exit points, such as the bulletin board problem discussed earlier. Different students may approach the problem differently, and achieve at least a partial solution to the problem (e.g. create at least one rectangle).

This has been discussed in other chapters in this book, but I also want to emphasize how lesson study does not mean one lesson. As I outlined in the previous paragraphs, the lesson presented in this example can be made into two lessons to produce more focused learning opportunities for the teachers. In Japan, lesson study often occurs as teachers plan an instructional unit together, as "*jugyo*" in "*jugyo kenkyuu*" ("lesson study" in Japanese) means both lesson and unit. Many experienced teachers globally already think of student learning as a trajectory, leading from one lesson to the next, not constrained in a short individual lesson. Thus, for lesson study, what is important is deciding which lesson of the unit is more suitable for a research lesson (revealing student thinking the most).

## Lesson study as research

Lesson study is a research process, and teachers identify and plan their own research to find answers to their research questions. As with any other research, careful planning makes the actual process go more smoothly and helps teachers better understand student learning of the topics in questions. I will outline the research process below as your team could follow it to make the experiences more meaningful.

### Step 1: choosing a topic

*What are challenging topics for students to learn at your grade level? What topics do you want to understand of student learning better? Are there topics you always wished there were better ways to teach? If so, student learning of the particular topic can be an ideal research lesson goal (in Step 2 below).*

In reflecting back on your experiences in classrooms, is there a topic (or two) that comes to your mind that your students usually find it hard to learn? Do you have a lesson that you feel you want to rush through so you don't have to answer students' questions? Is there a lesson in your new textbook curriculum that looks very different from what you have taught before that you wonder how to teach it?

*Meeting Tips*: Make a list of a few topics that come to mind, and share them in the lesson study team. If you teach different grade levels, you may need to provide background information (for example, what students have learned before, how this concept is used in later lessons) for your colleagues who teach different grades. Ask questions of your colleagues so they can expand on their reasoning. Focus the discussion on why you think the concept is difficult to learn, and explain the ways you have tried to teach it before. Identify typical difficulties you see with your students in detail. Is there a common topic or two in your team? If so, identify them as a possible research lesson topic. It can be a broad topic right now, as you will narrow it down gradually through the lesson study process later on to decide on a lesson goal (see Figure 2.4).

If you are working as a cross-grade team, try first to identify what concept may be relevant across grade levels so all of you can participate. In working with elementary school teachers with mathematics, we have found that topics such as subtraction (single and multiple digit), geometry (categorizing shapes), fractions (finding equivalence) and analyzing word problems worked well across grades.

### *Step 2: setting a lesson goal and planning a lesson*

*How can you make student thinking of the topic visible in the lesson? What are the essential struggles students have? What lessons have you taught on the topics before? How did your students think in the lesson? What specific part of the lesson did students surprise you with their thinking before?*

Once you decide on the possible general topic for the research lesson, share how you have taught the concept before with your colleagues, and discuss student struggles with learning the topic, with as much detail as possible. What kind of problems are particularly challenging for the students? Which lessons and activities did you find effective and why? Can you explain how your students learn the concept and what typical challenges are? Is there prerequisite understanding (what students need to know) before they can learn the concept?

---

**Case of Grade 5 lesson study on division of fractions - Identifying challenges:** As a fifth-grade teacher, Ellen dreads the lesson on division of fractions. She usually teaches these lessons quickly by going over the procedures of "flip top and bottom, multiply the top numbers, multiply the bottom numbers, and find the answer." Once or twice in her classrooms, different students asked why it worked that way, and she felt embarrassed that she did not have the answer. She simply responded, "It's just the way it is. You don't need to know why," while she wished she knew how to explain better.

In lesson study, she shared this experience with her colleagues, and was surprised that many of them also did not like this lesson. They discussed why this was challenging for students to learn, and thought students should simply memorize the steps and review multiplication facts. The lesson study facilitator asked if they knew anything about student thinking of division of fractions. Ellen and her colleagues only knew the procedural steps, and little idea how students thought of the concept. They identified this as a possible lesson study topic.

---

*Figure 2.4* Case box 1

*Meeting Tips*: Individually, take a few minutes to write answers to the questions above. In sharing with colleagues, add as much information as you can so they will understand where you are coming from. Keep in mind that for some challenging topics, you or your colleagues may only know procedural development (students learning steps of a solution method). Although mastering procedures is indeed important, ask yourselves if you knew how students would actually think as they solve the problem if a prescribed method is not given first. For your research lesson, you want to design a lesson activity which reveals *students' original thinking* (and not following given procedures).

Based on your answers to this question, you can start to think about the lesson goal. For example, the team may decide that place value is a challenging topic across multiple elementary school grade levels. In examining different lesson scenarios and curricular materials, you may agree that many students seem to struggle with the concept when they are initially learning to subtract double-digit numbers in the first grade. The team may come to the research lesson goal, "First-grade students will use 10s in solving subtraction problems," to further specify the problem situation in which the students are most likely to struggle; thus their learning will become visible in the research lesson (see Figure 2.5).

Read research articles on student learning of the topic. Examine different curricular materials that explain how students learn the topic.

*Meeting Tips*: Discuss in your group if the ideas presented in the readings make sense to you, if you have also seen similar thinking before. If not, why do you think you haven't? This may be a good place for you to go back to your classrooms and ask a handful of students to solve a problem or two from the readings (informal assessment). How do your students think?

Design a research lesson that makes students' original ideas come to the surface, so you can learn about student thinking of the topic. Use problems from the readings if you want to, or modify a lesson from conceptually sound textbook curricula. There is no need for you to plan a lesson from scratch (you are discouraged to do so). Start with a good lesson, and focus your effort on how to modify the original lesson for your own students. As a team, solve the

---

**Thinking Point 1: What are the differences between conceptual learning and procedural learning?**

In teaching mathematics, you are likely to support your students to develop understanding of concepts as well as to learn procedures to solve problems using the concepts. In good mathematics teaching, both of these are necessary.

1 Conceptual learning has to do with students understanding why of the concept. Why can a number be decomposed to different chunks and still make up the same number? Why can a fraction be represented with different models?
2 Procedural learning is how to find answers in the problem situations using the concept. How do we decompose a number into tens and ones to make the operation process easier? How can we find equivalent fractions by multiplying?

For research lessons, we want lesson activities to address the *why*. In well-planned research lessons, students' developing understanding is revealed in meaningful ways. You will not want to teach a lesson in which all students have correct answers. You will want the lesson in which a variation of partial understanding is revealed.

---

*Figure 2.5* Thinking point 1

> **Grade 5 case continued - Understanding challenges, student pre-assessment, curriculum study**
>
> As Ellen and her colleagues discussed division of fractions, it became clear that they only knew the procedural solutions of the operation but not why the procedure worked. The team could discuss their prior successes in terms of teaching procedures (e.g., teaching through mnemonic), but none of them taught the lesson conceptually before. They further realized that they have never learned it conceptually as students in elementary schools themselves, either. They had little ideas how students would think of the division of fractions situation if procedures were not taught first.
>
> The team read up on students' concept development, then tried some problems with a few students. They confirmed that their students also thought in similar ways as in these articles. That was a surprise. For some of the team members, it was the first time division of fractions was making sense. They looked at a lesson in a textbook curriculum that was recommended to them as highly conceptual. The unit in the curriculum started with reviewing division of whole numbers, then incorporated fractions gradually: whole number ÷ whole number (10 ÷ 5 = 2)→ fraction ÷ whole number (10/3 ÷5 = 2/3) → fraction ÷ unit fraction (10/3 ÷ 1/3 = 10) → fraction ÷ fraction 10/3 ÷ 2/3 = 5). This sequence made sense to the teachers, and they felt they could even explain why they were flip the top and bottom numbers for dividing.

*Figure 2.6* Case box 2

problem yourselves together, and anticipate how students would think in the lesson. Make a list of all possible student approaches and discuss them in detail. Are there connections among the approaches? How are they similar and different from one another? In the lesson, how do you plan to help students make connections among different ideas? See Figure 2.6.

*Step 3: planning data collection*

*How do you plan to collect student learning data in the research lesson? Given the goal of the lesson, how do you plan to investigate how students learn? Are the data closely related to the main lesson activity?*

Now that you have the draft of the lesson, think about where in the lesson student thinking becomes visible, as that is the place where you want to collect data. Think about the focal activity in the lesson with open-ended questions, in which you anticipated student responses. That may be a perfectly good place to collect data on student thinking. You don't need to have more than a couple of data collection points identified throughout the lesson. But these points are very important, as the data you collect will answer the questions you asked at the beginning of the lesson study process (student thinking of the concept you want to know more). Data can come in various forms: student solution strategies shown in their notebooks, posters created by student groups, or recorded student presentations and accompanying artefacts. The format of the data is less important than how you anticipate student responses in the data. Please take some time to collaboratively brainstorm different possibilities and how students will explain and show their thinking.

*Meeting Tips*: In your team, go over the lesson scenario one more time. Don't skip a step, and discuss each part of the lesson carefully. Review student thinking you anticipated and have different team members explain how students will think in the problem-solving process.

After reviewing the lesson, discuss what part of the lesson may reveal students' original thinking more clearly. Identify one or two places in the lesson plan and anticipate student thinking fully for these places again (see Figure 2.7).

Before finalizing the lesson, examine carefully how the three research points (goals of the lesson, lesson activity, data collection) are related. How does the lesson activity (directly) address the goal(s) of the lesson you specified? How do the data you are collecting during the research lesson directly relate to the lesson activity on what students learn? At this point, most lesson study teams fine-tune and reword the goal of the lesson to be more specific, to be targeted to student learning of a certain concept. Do not be afraid to have a very narrow and specific research lesson goal, as it only helps your investigation become deeper. Use the following table to contrast the three research points and tweak the lesson one more time if appropriate (see Figures 2.8 and 2.9).

## Step 4: debrief discussions

*Focus on the student learning data you collected and discuss relevant aspects of the lesson activities/problems and how the lesson helped students meet the lesson goals.*

If your lesson study team paid close attention to the alignment among (1) research lesson goals, (2) lesson activity/problem and (3) student learning data collected during the lesson, the debrief discussion will naturally focus on student learning revealed by the data you collected, illustrating how the lesson activity or problem effectively addressed the lesson goals you identified in the lesson study process, framing your students' learning experiences. The tighter the connections among these three points, the more seamlessly you would be able to see the relationships among them, thus the debriefing would go smoothly. If at this point you are not sure about what students learned in the lesson, reflect on the connections among the three points again, identify the possible misalignment and make decisions as to what you would do in the next lesson study cycle to make the connections tighter (see Figure 2.10).

---

**Grade 5 case continued – Deciding on the data to collect**

Ellen and her colleagues anticipated student thinking of division of fractions multiple times. By doing so, they came to see how the gradual incorporation of fractions in the division problem sequence helped make the connections between different problem types. As data collection points, the team decided that they wanted to know how students would approach fraction ÷ fraction problem when it was introduced in the lesson. They wanted to know the strategies students develop through the sequence of problems prior to fraction ÷ fraction problem (whole number ÷ whole number → fraction ÷ whole number → fraction ÷ unit fraction) may be extended to the new type of problems. They especially wanted to know how students might reason the operation process with fractions.

---

*Figure 2.7* Case box 3

| Goals of the lesson | Lesson activity | Data collection |
|---|---|---|
| | | |

*Figure 2.8* Lesson plan format

> **Grade 5 case continued – Finalizing the lesson**
>
> Ellen and the colleagues reviewed the lesson plan one more time to make sure research process is streamlined and meaningful. Once they revisited the lesson goal they had identified many weeks ago (students will learn how to divide fractions), they realized that it was too broad for the actual lesson they developed, thus they revised it as: "students will extend their understanding of whole number division to divide fractions," as the extension part was important in their investigation. They also tweaked the wording for the data collection slightly to fit better with the research process.
>
> | Goals of the lesson | Lesson activity | Data collection points |
> | --- | --- | --- |
> | Students will extend their understanding of whole number division to divide fractions. | Students will solve a set of division problems (finding amount of paint) with changing natures of quantities:<br><br>1) whole number ÷ whole number ($10 \div 5 = 2$)<br>→ 2) fraction ÷ whole number ($10/3 \div 5 = 2/3$)<br>→ 3) fraction ÷ unit fraction ($10/3 \div 1/3 = 10$)<br>→ 4) fraction ÷ fraction ($10/3 \div 2/3 = 5$) | When the final problem is presented that requires students to divide fraction by fraction, how do they extend the strategies they used so far to solve the problem? |

*Figure 2.9* Case box 4

> **Thinking Point 2: Is your lesson open-ended enough?**
>
> If you want to see how your students truly think, the lesson has to be open-ended to invite different student thinking. Open-ended lesson means the problem
>
> 1) is presented without prescribed solution first;
> 2) is new to the students (they have never solved a problem like that before) while they can use what they have learned before to try to solve the problem; and
> 3) can be solved in multiple ways, by students attempting to use their prior knowledge.
>
> You may anticipate many different student responses for an open-ended problem.
>
> Examples of open-ended and close-ended problems:
>
> Open: Make a story problem that goes with the equation $10 + 5 = 15$.
> Close: What is the answer of $10 + 5$?
> Open: Find as many ways as possible to make 24.
> Close: Which is bigger, $6 \times 4$ or $5 \times 7$?
>
> Note: Close-ended problems can be made open-ended simply by adding, "Explain your thinking" at the end. For example, for the close-ended problem examples above, student explanations will typically vary and create additional space to show different thinking.

*Figure 2.10* Thinking point 2

## Summary and conclusion

As discussed in this chapter, the importance of the research process in lesson study cannot be emphasized enough. You are asking a question (about student learning) to understand better how students learn so you can better teach the concepts for them. The ways in which the lesson reveals student thinking process, bringing out typical confusions and challenges, is the basis of the research process, and the lesson goal is to help students navigate the process in the lesson. Paying attention to how the three research points are related throughout your lesson study process will help ensure your own learning as teachers, bringing actual student learning central in the lesson and providing a lot of important new ideas about student learning and teaching.

By identifying meaningful lesson study goals, lesson activity and student learning data to be collected, you are extending your expertise. You will also enjoy the collaborative process that pushes the effort as a global teacher professional community, supporting each other in developing the new knowledge about student learning.

Maintaining the researchers' stance is important, positioning you as a researcher in the education field to improve instructional practices. Your work means more than just what happens in your classroom, and what you learn in lesson study has a broader implication for other teachers and their students' learning. You are an expert in learning, and your classroom is a research lab where you can investigate it. If the teacher professional community takes on a collective pride with this researcher identity, our ways of thinking about teaching and learning will shift positively. In different countries, such as in Japan and Finland, teachers are already considered as teacher researchers, and they engage in classroom-based research as a part of daily work. In other countries, such as the United States, it may require a fundamental shift in our thinking, yet in order to make a strong and broader impact, streamlining the research process in instruction as discussed in this chapter becomes crucial.

## Additional readings

Clarke, D., Mesiti, C., Jablonka, E., & Shimizu, Y. (2006). Addressing the challenge of legitimate international comparisons: Lesson structure in the USA, Germany, and Japan. In D. J. Clarke, J. Emanuelson, E. Jablonka, & I.A.C. Mok (Eds.), *Making connections: Comparing mathematics classrooms around the world* (pp. 23–45). Rotterdam: Sense.

Hiebert, J., Morris, A. K., & Glass, B. (2003). Learning to learn to teach: An "experiment" model for teaching and teacher preparation in mathematics. *Journal of Mathematics Teacher Education*, *6*, 201–222.

Lewis, C., & Tsuchida, I. (1998, Winter). A lesson is like a swiftly flowing river: Research lessons and the improvement of Japanese education. *American Educator*, *22*, 14–17, 50–52.

Murata, A. (2011). Conceptual overview of lesson study: Introduction. In L. Hart, A. Alston, & A. Murata (Eds.), *Lesson study research and practice in mathematics education: Learning together* (pp. 1–12). New York, NY: Springer.

Murata, A., Bofferding, L., Pothen, B., Taylor, M., & Wischnia, S. (2012). Making connections among student learning, content, and teaching: Teacher talk paths in elementary mathematics lesson study. *Journal for Research in Mathematics Education*, *43*(5), 616–650.

Stigler, J. W., & Hiebert, J. (1999). *The teaching gap: Best ideas from the world's teachers for improving education in the classroom*. New York, NY: Free Press.

# 3 How case pupils, pupil interviews and sequenced research lessons can strengthen teacher insights in *how* to improve learning for all pupils

*Peter Dudley and Jean Lang*

This chapter focuses on ways of helping teachers see and understand more about how their pupils are learning in their lesson studies. We will start by describing the role of "case pupils" and then go on to describe the use of pupil interviews and sequences of research lessons in enhancing what can be learned from and then gained for the case pupils themselves and other pupils they represent. In the following four speech bubbles are snippets from the post research lesson discussions of teachers in three primary schools using lesson study (LS) to improve the way their children learn mathematics (see Figures 3.1 and 3.2).

> (We invite you to interact with us once or twice in this chapter with these)
> Let's begin with some detective work! Read each speech bubble and try to work out from the discussion what aspects of teaching mathematics the lesson study was trying to develop. Jot down your thoughts as well as any questions you have.

*Figure 3.1* Thinking point 1

> T1 Hailey was much more confident talking with .. the [lesson] starter [activity] …
> T2 With the bigger numbers?
> T1 That's it yeah. Yeah. ….
> T3 She even challenged herself with the extension activity to, you know, write in words. She was very keen to try and do that.
> T2. Yeah. Bradley also said that he felt much more confident with that, and so even though it was only a starter, I think it was good….
> T3. Because that *was built on from last [research] lesson..*
> T3 *..and that was something that was identified; that we wanted to focus on*. Even though it was just a starter *it was linked*. Francesca I thought was.. trying with the extension task as well, to write the words ..um ..and she was quite confident in reading back to the class.
> T1 Yeh.
> T3..I think out of all three of them she probably ..was most confident and …
> T2 (Interrupting) It's *really* nice to see! Because in September she was, like, *very* quiet and lacking in confidence. So she's really come out of herself.

*Figure 3.2* School A: post research lesson 2 discussion

*How to improve learning for all pupils* 15

The LS variant in use in these examples is Research Lesson Study (RLS) (Dudley, 2014), which usually uses sequences of three research lessons. Each sequence develops skills or deepens understanding in an aspect of learning the LS group has identified as needing improvement. However, you can use the ideas we discuss in this chapter in any form of lesson or learning study. Case pupils are identified for particular focus in these research lessons (see Figure 3.3).

These snippets are taken from discussions that follow the second or third research lesson in each school's sequence, where before reaching broader conclusions about what has worked in the research lesson and for which pupils they discuss what each teacher observed and noted about precisely how the three case pupils progressed in the lesson in comparison with predictions made by the lesson study group when they were planning the lesson (see Figure 3.4).

> T1. Yes, .. I was watching Maryam at that point. [When we planned the lesson] we were hoping she'd sort of take her time and go back to the visuals and stuff. And um, she set about ordering the numbers. She wrote them down. ..The very first thing she DID do was to go to the tenths and she said: 'I knew I had to look at the tenths first because it was the biggest' and then she corrected herself and said '*greatest* value' (so the vocabulary's starting to come!!) ..er and she said 'I know that because I remember from the size of the objects we used.' So, in terms of what we had [predicted] she would do, she absolutely *did* do. And then .. she said 'I started to put the ones with the three decimal places as the biggest… but then I remembered to check the tenths first.'
> T2. Mmm!
> T1. So for *me*, she definitely benefited from the work that we'd done before..
> T3. That's great! Definite progress.
> T2. And one thing I noticed.. one thing I'm pleased, when it comes to Maryam, is… that self-belief! The confidence she how has! She sort of lacked the stamina in the past but now she's willing to have a go and she's able to succeed at it with a bit of prompting.

*Figure 3.3* School B: post research lesson 3 discussion

> T1. And then……. Rizwan?
> T2. It was interesting, because he was looking at the visual for equivalent fractions and he was looking at two quarters and a half, and he said 'Oh look! They are exactly the same!' And Luke went 'Yeah! Because they're "equivalent," That's two quarters. And that's a half.' But it's interesting for Rizwan because he was 'Oh yeahyeahyeah' *but* he HADN'T got that concept that they look the same!
> T3 Hmmm! He's probably used to the numbers..
> T1...the numbers!
> T3 ..when you work it out.
> T2 But he VISUALLY was surprised that they *looked* equivalent!
> T1. Hmm!

*Figure 3.4* School C: post research lesson 3 discussion

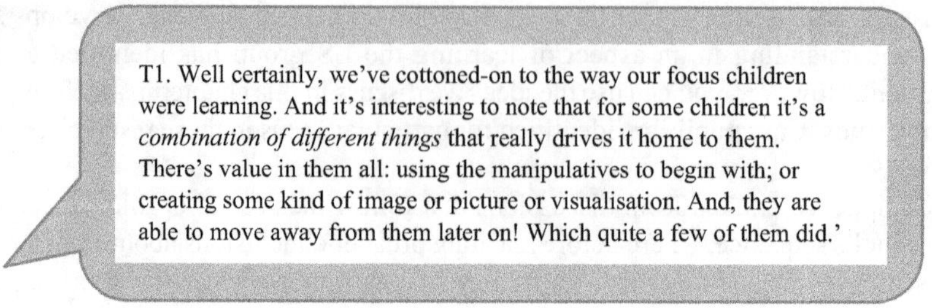

> T1. Well certainly, we've cottoned-on to the way our focus children were learning. And it's interesting to note that for some children it's a *combination of different things* that really drives it home to them. There's value in them all: using the manipulatives to begin with; or creating some kind of image or picture or visualisation. And, they are able to move away from them later on! Which quite a few of them did.'

*Figure 3.5* School B: post research lesson 3 discussion

The teachers had been experimenting with using manipulatives or with processes of visualization to build aspects of their pupils' understanding of the mathematical concepts they were learning about, rather than relying too heavily on procedure (see Figure 3.5).

You can tell from these discussions that while many pupils were able to learn more or less as predicted, some clearly did not do so, while others surprised their teachers by exceeding their predictions.

A growing body of research demonstrates that, as adults, we tend to see what we expect to see unless something forces us to notice that things are not as we assumed. Learning to notice in this way is an important component of professional expertise (Bransford, Brown, & Cocking, 2000). For teachers, the busy, unpredictable and complex nature of the classroom often means that we tend not to "see" our pupils very clearly at all. Instead we teach constructs (our assumptions) of where we believe our pupils to be in their learning at the time. The snippet dialogues suggest several instances of this happening. For example, they suggest that Rizwan and Bradley (and other pupils like them) will benefit in future from being able to visualize concepts in mathematics learning, and it seems that this realization was a welcome surprise for the teachers.

The sharp-eyed reader will also have picked up that these teachers seem not only to have been paying close observational attention to these pupils as they learned in the research lessons, but also that they seem to have had discussions with them about their learning. Post-lesson pupil interviews are also an important component of RLS. Pupils tend to be very pleased that their teachers are studying their learning in order to try and improve it and, being experienced lesson observers themselves – as learners – they can often provide "pupil's-eye view" insights into what they (and pupils like them) particularly benefitted from or struggled with in a research lesson (Dudley, 2013).

Of course, the knowledge gained from the case pupil prediction/observations and the pupil interviews is essentially formative or diagnostic. It invites further experimentation to explore whether the suggested refinements for future teaching actually result in the anticipated benefits to pupils' learning.

When developing LS in English classrooms, many teachers involved in a national pilot (Dudley, 2013) incorporated these specific elements to counter the effects of these challenges. They were designed to help lesson study group teachers jointly to:

- See actual pupils rather than psychological constructs for them;
- Identify how stages of planned progress towards the object of learning in a research lesson manifest themselves and are recognisable in what pupils say or do;

*How to improve learning for all pupils* 17

- Explore evidence and hypothesize why pupils did or did not learn as designed;
- Seek out and test potentially fruitful alternative teaching approaches for future research lessons and subsequent teaching.

"Exploratory talk" is a term that describes modes of discussion between collaborative learners engaged in solving problems together, which enable the group members to connect their emerging ideas and to harness their collective brain power by "inter-thinking" (Barnes & Todd, 1977; Mercer, 1995; Mercer, 2000). Because most teacher learning in lesson studies is accomplished through inter-thinking through exploratory talk by the lesson study group teachers (Dudley, 2013), we have developed ground rules to optimize their learning through such group discussion. Ground rules (Mercer, 2000) to guide lesson study group teachers' exploratory talk in important stages of the post-research lesson or planning discussion process can strengthen collaborative *teacher learning* and thus generate ever-improving pupil learning. Examples of such ground rules for teacher talk are given throughout the sections that follow.

In this chapter we will use examples from lesson studies that have taken place in schools and pre-school settings in order to exemplify and demonstrate the value that a focus on case pupils, pupil interviews and sequenced research lessons can add to:

- Teachers' learning;
- School case knowledge;
- Practice, pedagogy, curriculum and teaching that better meets the learners' needs;
- Leadership of the school.

We will provide advice on effective practice to help you to ensure that your learning is enriched and strengthened throughout the stages of a lesson study cycle. These stages are set out in Figure 3.6). Although these relate to RLS, they can be incorporated into any LS approach.

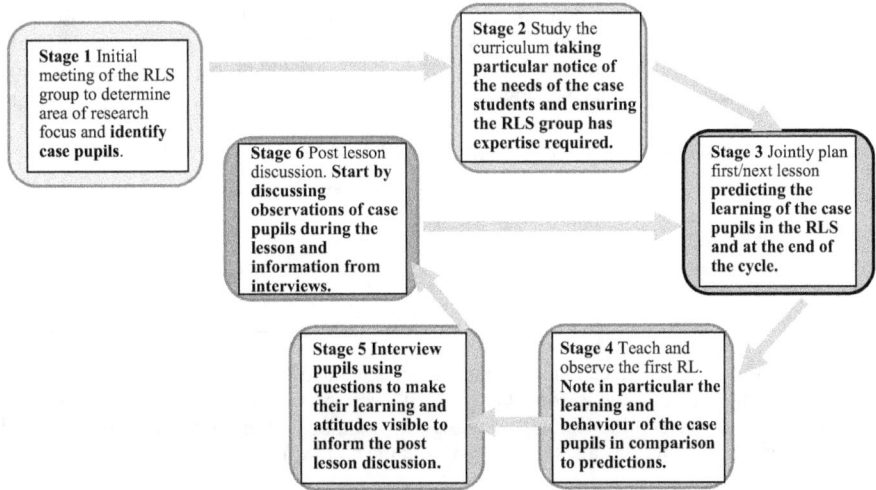

*Figure 3.6* Stages in the lesson study process emphasizing the role of case pupils

## Who are case pupils?

Case pupils may represent different groups of learners in the class. If a new way of teaching an aspect of curriculum is being introduced to the class, then the case pupils selected may represent (1) pupils likely to find this approach easy, (2) pupils who may struggle but ultimately succeed and (3) pupils who may require additional teaching or support in order to succeed. If, however, the lesson study is focusing on a particular learner group that is struggling in a curriculum area, then the case pupils will be chosen from within that group of learners (see Figure 3.7).

A lesson study group will identify (typically two or three) phases in the RL when they will be waiting for pupils to complete a task before starting the next phase. It is at the end of each of these phases that they must agree and record on their research lesson (RL) plan what they predict each case student will need to have said, written, or drawn *in order to reveal that she or he is ready to move on to the next phase of the lesson* (see detailed guidance on stage 3 below). Reaching this consensus is a "ground rule for teacher talk" in RLS.

Dudley, Xu, and Lang (2019) describe how the use of this ground rule often exposes considerable differences between the initial expectations of the members of the LS group in relation to the predicted student behaviour and also in relation to the precise nature of the lesson's object of learning. These are only resolved through further discussion and exploratory talk.

We will now take you through the lesson study stages and use examples to guide you in how to get the most from the use of case pupils, pupil interviews and sequenced research lessons (see Figure 3.8).

### *Stage 1: initial meeting of the RLS group*

*How to identify the best case pupils for a specific lesson study*

---

Imagine you are about to conduct a RL with a class you regularly teach. In the RL you will be introducing and trying out a new approach to teaching an aspect of the curriculum that you have not used before, but which your review of curriculum and learning suggests may address difficulties encountered by some pupils in learning this curriculum content (which could be knowledge, skills or other understanding).

Which of your current real-life students might you consider to be case students – and why?

---

*Figure 3.7* Thinking point 2

---

Think of a lesson you will teach in the next day or so and a particular child in the class. Identify one or two of the phases of the lesson when you will need to know whether certain children are ready for the next phase of the lesson to start. What would be your predictions be for the child you have identified if this was a research lesson and the child was a case pupil?

---

*Figure 3.8* Thinking point 3

It is at this meeting that you identify (usually) three pupils who might typify different groups of learners in the class (see Figure 3.9). These could be pupils who are making good, average or below average progress either in the lesson study subject or in a cross-curricular skill (such as academic writing). Or they could be pupils who are not learning or engaging perhaps as well as you would hope in this aspect of learning.

Your choice of case pupils will help you to collect evidence to support your research to ensure you discuss what you know already about any misconceptions these pupils might already have which could affect their learning and which will need to be addressed through the lesson study.

## *Stage 2: studying the curriculum, teaching materials and research*

*How can you use your research of curriculum and learning resources to identify strategies to improve teaching and learning to meet the needs of the case pupils? And how do you ensure that your team has the necessary expertise to plan effective lessons?*

Research should focus on identifying and discussing strategies which could improve learning for the case pupils in the focus curriculum area, taking into account your own school context (see Figure 3.10). It is important for the research team to have sufficient expertise in the focus curriculum area as well as in any specific needs of the case pupils. For example, if a case pupil is learning the language of instruction *as a second language*, then the team should include someone who has knowledge and experience of pedagogical and linguistic approaches to best support their learning and language acquisition.

## *Stage 3: joint planning of the first lesson*

*How do you make sure that your planning supports your collection of evidence of learning by the case pupils?*

> A group of teachers working in a nursery wanted to focus on developing characteristics of effective learning of children aged three and four. They identified case children representing the demographics of the setting, and focused on different heritage groups, one with a white British background, one Black Caribbean and one Somali child.

*Figure 3.9* Example 1

> One special school in London included an expert in Dyscalculia in their Lesson Study team to establish their understanding of the way that pupils thought about estimation of number, and to analyse what experiences they might need to develop this particular concept.

*Figure 3.10* Example 2

Write out in full what you want your pupils to be able to do with their new knowledge by the end of the research lesson.

Note what you predict the response of each case pupil will be: what do you predict that each case pupil will be doing at each development phase in the research lesson that would give you evidence that their progress in the lesson is going according to plan?

Agree who will focus their attentions on which case pupil(s). It helps to agree on this to ensure that you don't all gather data about two pupils and miss the third. Have a reserve case pupil in case one is absent on the day.

It is a good idea to try out tasks in advance as part of your planning to help you anticipate pupil learning. Some teachers carry out a "mock-up" lesson with colleagues playing the case pupils (Lewis, Friedkin, Emerson, Henn, & Goldsmith, 2019). In RLS, teachers often collectively imagine and role-play short sections of lessons which can allow usually invisible, *tacit* teaching knowledge to surface and strengthen the knowledge that informs the next research lesson (Dudley, 2013) (see Figure 3.11).

## *Stage 4: teach and observe the first research lesson*

*How do you make sure that the team reflects on the predictions of case pupil learning and behaviour at the significant points identified in the research lesson rather than focuses on teaching?*

It is really important that the group refers to what they predicted each pupil would be doing at each stage of the lesson in their planning and what supporting evidence they will be looking for to reveal whether this is indeed happening. The focus of the observers should be on pupils' learning and not on the teacher (who is, after all, teaching something they have all planned and agreed). A good idea is that they alternate their focus in the research lesson between *zooming in* on the case pupil(s) and then *panning back out* to look across the whole class to observe what is happening more widely.

Observers should try to capture the case pupils' responses at predicted points in the lesson and note how they match or differ from the predictions. They should also note any critical incidents observed or whether there are any common patterns (for example, all case pupils misunderstand something in the same way) (see Figure 3.12).

---

A research team in a primary school in London focussed their study on deepening pupils' conceptual understanding of decimal fractions. In their first RL they wanted the pupils to be able to explain how 1/10, 1/100 and 1/1000 could be made from a given unit (base10). They identified three significant parts of the lesson to observe and predicted the learning and behaviour of the case pupils within each activity:

i) They wanted to observe the pupils' exploratory talk in order to identify their understanding of the whole, tenths and hundreds.
ii) In the second activity the pupils were presented with a new whole (base ten large cube) and the group wanted to find out whether the pupils could extend their knowledge of decimal fractions and work out that the small cubes would be thousands.
iii) The third activity observed involved the pupils in recording units, tens, hundreds and thousands on a grid using the base 10 objects and using this visual to determine which had the greatest value (by comparing the size of the decimal parts).

---

*Figure 3.11* Example 3

> Teachers from a modern foreign languages (MFL) department in an English secondary school identified a significant drop in the performance of pupils in reading and so focussed their lesson study on the development of strategies to encourage learners' confidence in comprehending text written in a foreign language. In the first RL, pupils were provided with traditional reading tasks and observed following the text instructions. Observers identified that the lower and middle attaining case pupils were struggling with this task and the interviews that followed confirmed this. The team used this RL as reconnaissance, acting as a baseline to identify barriers to learning and to apply knowledge gained to plan strategies to support these pupil's learning the following two RLs in which, as a result, pupils employed a toolkit of metacognitive strategies aimed at developing confidence in approaching reading comprehension. Following the second and third RLs, the team were able to confirm predictions that, for example, the lower attaining case pupil was able to annotate his text, identify the verbs, work out the tenses and conjugation even when a verb was unknown. Analysing the techniques, skills and strategies that might had not come naturally to one learner encouraged teachers to explicitly include them in lessons across all languages taught in the school. Designing reading activities based on academic research that matched the observed learning needs of these case pupils, had thus enabled teachers to adjust existing texts and strategies to help meet the needs of all pupils.

*Figure 3.12* Example 4

## *Stage 5: conducting pupil interviews*

*How to conduct post research lesson pupil interviews that can enhance your insight into pupil learning in research lessons.*

Pupil interviews were introduced as a result of compelling research by Ruddock (1996), McIntyre, Pedder and Ruddock (2005) and others, revealing the benefits for students, teachers and schools of giving students greater voice and agency in their learning and schooling. The "ground rules for talk" in these interview discussions suggest that interviewers ask the students to imagine the teachers are to conduct the RL again the following day with a similar class of students and to advise their teachers what might be changed in the lesson and why (Dudley, 2014). A discussion usually ensues which is both revealing to the LS group about aspects of their RL and which is also formative and of practical use.

While these interviews provide lesson study group members with insights into the perceptions students have about what helped them learn as well as what hindered them (Warwick et al., 2019), a common opportunity that is missed by lesson study groups is that of tailoring their interview questions closely to the research lesson itself. There is little time between the end of the RL and the student interview which usually immediately follows (prior to the post lesson discussion).

The group of pupils selected for interview may or may not include case pupils. Often (as can be seen in the previous snippets), one or two case pupils are amongst the group interviewed.

The interview should be short (no more than five minutes) and can be done with all the pupils in a group or individually.

Try to conduct the interview as soon as possible, ideally at the end of the lesson, and try to capture some of the pupils' exact words in your notes (see Figures 3.13 and 3.14).

> Think of a lesson you have taught recently where you have tried out a new approach aimed at improving motivation, engagement and learning. What questions to pupils would have helped you to evaluate the success of the approach from their perspectives?
>
> How could you create an atmosphere conducive to honest feedback?

*Figure 3.13* Thinking point 4

> Teachers in a primary school found that pupils were initially quite reticent about feeding back about their learning especially when what they wanted to say might seem critical of their teachers or, for similar reasons, if they had ideas about making a lesson better. This changed as soon as the pupils saw that their responses were leading to pedagogical changes, making it clear that their opinions were valued by their teachers. This school has now built this use of pupil voice into the school's improvement processes. It is now an accepted and valued strategy across the whole school.

*Figure 3.14* Example 5

> The first post lesson discussion often provides the lesson study research group with many surprises about the learning of their case pupils. They notice big differences between their assumptions about the pupils as learners and what they observed in practice. The research team in **Example 3** (above) found that their case pupils had learnt 'correct' mathematics procedures without really knowing how they work so that they were unable to apply the procedure in a situation other than the context in which it was learnt. The use of manipulatives in the lesson study played a significant role in the pupils' construction of meaningful mathematical ideas and concepts. The school concluded that manipulatives should be used before formal symbolic instruction and this has now been built into the school's mathematics policy.

*Figure 3.15* Example 6

### Stage 6: post lesson discussion

*How does a focus on case pupils help to ensure that the post lesson discussion focuses on learning rather than teaching?*

Here, another ground rule for talk comes into play. The flow of the discussion needs to begin with each teacher's observations of the case pupils, of how closely their observed learning matched the group's predictions, and their responses to the lesson shared through pupil interviews (see Figure 3.15).

This ground rule discussion process preserves the group's focus on pupil learning and on the teacher learning that arises from this. It thus reduces any tendency for the discussion to turn into judgemental feedback on teaching, which so often kills teacher learning before it has begun.

Notes (provided in Table 3.1) from the first post-lesson discussion of the lesson study group featured in Example 3 reflect how this ground rule can ensure that the team focuses on the learning from case pupils *before* they consider any teaching approaches. The prompts to the left of the notes help to ensure that the group considers the learning not only of the case pupils but of all pupils in the group and acts as a guide to analysis of the lesson for the teachers. You can also see how the data collected from the case pupils influenced their subsequent planning of the second research lesson.

*Table 3.1* Post lesson discussion record RL1 (the LS group's agreed notes)

| | |
|---|---|
| What progress did each case pupil make? Was this enough? | **Case pupil A**: M really benefitted from the use of the manipulatives and the partner talk. In the post lesson discussion, she explained that she likes it when someone her own age explains "stuff because it gets in her head". M certainly developed her conceptual understanding through the lesson. She explained that before, she didn't understand why thousandths were smaller than hundredths, but that she "gets it now". |
| | **Case pupil B**: S was initially confused with the difference in relative size. She struggled to articulate why a tenth is a tenth and a hundredth is a hundredth. However, with the help of her partner and through directed questioning from the teacher, her conceptual understanding and confidence grew. She did make progress in this lesson and I think we are clear about S's next steps. |
| | **Case Pupil C**: The gaps in R's conceptual understanding were evident in the exploratory talk section of the lesson. He needed the guidance from his partner to understand how to divide the whole into tenths, hundredths and thousandths. However, we did notice that through the manipulation of the resources he was more confident in showing decimal fractions at the end of the lesson. |
| What about others in the groups they typify? | All learners seemed to benefit from the use of the concrete materials. Through the hands-on manipulation of the resources, the children were better able to understand the relative size of each of the parts of the whole. In the post lesson feedback from the children, all of them seemed to have a more secure understanding of the basics of decimal fractions; in particular the value of each number in a decimal. |
| Do we need to revise our assessment of any pupils? | As this was the first lesson in the sequence, we planned this as a reconnaissance lesson, and I think there were good opportunities to assess the children's understanding in the lesson we planned. Through our probing questions and listening in to the children's exploratory talk, we were able to assess the children's conceptual understanding. In the next lesson we also need to build in some independent activities so we can continue to assess the individual children's understanding. |
| How did the teaching being developed help or hinder the pupils' learning? (Maybe a bit of both?) | **Case pupil A**: M was very clear in the post lesson discussion about the benefits of using the concrete materials and discussion with her partner. M showed increased confidence by the end of this lesson, and we need to build on this in the next lesson. |
| What surprises were there? Did we find out anything of note about the way they were learning? | **Case pupil B**: S definitely benefitted from the talk and the support of her partner. It was hugely beneficial that the class teacher took the time to think carefully about the mixed ability pairings. We were surprised and pleased to see S showing increasing confidence in her discussions with her partner. |
| | **Case pupil C**: R is normally very confident in the procedural side of maths, but it was surprising to see how much he struggled in this lesson. It was interesting to see the gaps in his conceptual understanding of fractional decimals. He certainly benefitted from the use of concrete materials and partner talk. |
| What aspect(s) of our teaching could be adjusted next time to improve the progress of our case pupils and all pupils? | We could have modelled the exploratory talk more explicitly, as some pairs struggled to sustain the conversation themselves. |
| | We will need to recap very explicitly on the new/improved understanding of decimal fractions from the first lesson. |

*(Continued)*

Table 3.1 (Continued)

| | |
|---|---|
| | We will allow partner talk before asking pupils to demonstrate the understanding using base ten equipment. |
| | We will incorporate the use of diagrammatic representation of decimal fractions and symbolic representation alongside the concrete apparatus during this lesson and hopefully strengthen the visual representation of decimal fractions before moving on to purely symbolic representation. |
| | Continue to allow partner talk as all of our focus children have said that they like the opportunity to talk with a partner in maths to help them understand better (either by teaching it to a peer or by having it explained by a peer). |
| So, what should we try next time? | Make sure we have a model of the whole that will break up into tenths and a model of the whole that will break up into hundredths. |
| | Get the children to demonstrate the relationship between the tenths, hundredths and thousandths by dividing each of these into ten. |
| | Move the children away from the concrete to the visual and finally the symbolic once their understanding is secure, but encourage children to use apparatus or diagrams if they feel they need them. |
| | Introduce the decimal parts of length using a meter tape that can be cut up into its decimal parts. |

### *Sequenced research lessons*

*How to build on discoveries made in each of a sequence of research lessons about how your teaching has affected your pupils' learning and how to develop, refine and test these in order to develop new pedagogical content knowledge that others can use.*

Table 3.1 also shows how each successive research lesson is dependent upon the findings of its predecessor. In fact, as teachers discuss each case student's learning in turn, they begin to realize what may be needed in the next research lesson which, thus, has its genesis in the analysis and findings of its predecessor.

Usually the first research lesson reveals more about gaps in teachers' knowledge of their pupils learning than it does about the content of the research lesson. Sometimes teachers use the first research lesson as a reconnaissance exercise precisely for this reason (as seen earlier in Example 3). The second research lesson is usually an opportunity to recalibrate and retry ideas in the new lesson on the basis of better knowledge of how pupils actually learned from the previous lesson. Often by the third research lesson there are one or two ideas that you wish to try out again for confirmation. But there will still be new approaches to be researched and trialled for those children whose needs you have yet to properly diagnose or meet.

So, these are not iterations of an identical lesson with the same intended learning outcome. They are sequences of different lessons that introduce, develop and embed particular skills and knowledge throughout the sequence. RLS thus combines lesson study, action research and design study. Design study is a science that is used when the safety of participants is paramount. It is used, for example, to improve aircraft engineering in series of design, trial and review flights. For this reason, lesson study is a good example of what is now called "improvement science".

## Conclusion

The use of case pupils, pupil interviews, sequenced research lessons and ground rules for teacher-talk discussed in this chapter have proved particularly helpful in guiding lesson study in the UK during a ten-year period of austerity when school finances have been cut in real terms. Indeed, we believe these approaches have helped to provide structure for professional learning within lesson study that teachers and school leaders can use together to collaboratively manage and indeed to develop their shared expertise and efficacy without constant need for external support or expertise.

At their best, these approaches help create lesson studies that are safe spaces for teachers to take risks, disclose uncertainties and try out new ideas – their own ideas informed by their research. For this reason there are many examples of teachers carrying out lesson studies because they want to do so, because it is fulfilling and because it improves their practice (Dudley et al., 2019).

Brave school leaders are using lesson study reports and presentations not only to improve learning for pupils but to act as drivers for improving teaching in their schools, precisely because while teachers are understandably fearful of judgement-laden appraisals and inspections, they are conversely enthusiastic about sharing the way they have improved the learning of their pupils through lesson studies. We believe that it is the deep grounding of first-hand knowledge through repeated analysis of fine-grained learning improvements of case pupils that helps give teachers this confidence.

However, we are also aware of instances where these approaches have sometimes backfired, where too much focus and attention has been paid, for example, to the case pupils at the expense of others. Case pupils should be representatives of typical learner groups in a subject area in a class. The secret in using case pupils is not only to improve their learning but also the learning of pupils with similar needs. We therefore advocate, for example, that novice teachers do not conduct lesson studies solely with other novice teachers if the opportunity exists to do so with more experienced colleagues who have greater reserves of professional knowledge and experience on which to draw. These issues are mostly common sense. However, if as a leader you judge that the necessary expertise in an area of development does not exist in your school, then it is essential to seek outside expert input to your lesson studies.

With these caveats, we believe that these features of RLS can be usefully added when needed to many models of lesson or learning study to help train skills in noticing, anticipating student responses, developing fruitful exploratory talk amongst the lesson study group, surfacing tacit teaching knowledge, and developing and co-evolving practice or pedagogical content knowledge of teachers over sequences of lessons. Once these formats have been internalized by the teachers involved and expert knowledge is developed, rigidity can in future give way to judicious selection or omission of such approaches as part of the normal course of teaching.

## Additional readings

Barnes, D., & Todd, F. (1977). *Communication and learning in small groups*. London: Routledge & Kegan Paul.

Bransford, D. J., Brown, A. L., & Cocking, R. R. (2000). *How people learn: Brain, mind, experience and school*. New York, NY: National Academy Press.

Dudley, P. (2013). Teacher learning in lesson study: What interaction-level discourse analysis revealed about how teachers utilised imagination, tacit knowledge of teaching and fresh evidence of students' learning, to develop practice knowledge and so enhance their students' learning. *Teaching and Teacher Education, 34*, 107–121.

Dudley, P. (2014). *Research lesson study: A handbook*. Retrieved from www.lessonstudy.co.uk

Dudley, P., Xu, H., Vermunt, JD., and Lang, J. (2019). Empirical evidence of the impact of lesson study on: Students' achievement, teachers' professional learning and on institutional and system evolution: An illustrative, complex case-development exemplar in London. *European Journal of Education*.

Lewis, C., Friedkin, S., Emerson, K., Henn, L., & Goldsmith, L. (2019). How does lesson study work? Towards a theory of lesson study process and impact. In R. Huang, A. Takahashi, & J. P. da Ponte (Eds.), *Theory and practice of lesson study in mathematics* (pp. 13–38). Springer.

McIntyre, D., Pedder, D., & Rudduck, J. (2005). Pupil voice: comfortable and uncomfortable learnings for teachers. *Research Papers in Education, 20*(2), 149–168.

Mercer, N. (1995). *The guided construction of knowledge: Talk amongst Teachers and Learners*. Clevedon: Multilingual Matters.

Mercer, N. (2000). *Words and minds: How we use language to think together*. London: Routledge.

Rudduck, J., Chaplain, R., & Wallace, G. (Eds ). (1996). *School improvement: what can pupils tell us?* London: David Fulton.

Warwick, P., Vrikki, M., Faeroyvik Karlson, A., Dudley, P., & Vermunt, J. (2018). The role of pupil voice as a trigger for teacher learning in lesson study professional groups. *Cambridge Journal of Education*. Retrieved from www.tandfonline.com/doi/full/10.1080/0305764X.2018.1556606

Warwick, P., Vrikki, M., Færøyvik Karlsen, A.M., Dudley, P., & Vermunt, J.D. (2019). The role of pupil voice as a trigger for teacher learning in lesson study professional groups. *Cambridge Journal of Education* 49(4):435–455, 04 July 2019.

# 4 Teacher learning through seeing students' mistakes during inclusive mathematics lesson study

*Judith Fabrega*

## Introduction

Examining students' thinking and mistakes can productively inform instructional decisions made during lesson study. While the connection between student thinking and instruction develops through the whole lesson study cycle, it indeed starts at the planning phase when an inclusive open-ended activity is examined, then the anticipated thinking is actually experienced in the lesson, followed by the connection being further strengthened while teachers analyze the effectiveness of the teaching choices during the debriefing.

While planning a mathematics lesson, a lesson study team (1) examines which elements of the lesson would engage students with different strategies to show their ideas, (2) anticipates students' levels of understanding and plans for responsive instruction and (3) discusses how to develop a sharper and focused observation for understanding how students think mathematically in research lessons. In order to support students developing their own mathematical understanding, instruction should be based on, take advantage of, and be aligned with students' own inventive problem-solving thinking. That means you could build from concepts and skills that students use when starting to solve a mathematical problem and help them move through the different levels of development, evaluating students' progress during the sequence. At the same time, this can also mean that the lesson incorporates open-ended and inclusive mathematical activities to allow students to start with what they already know, develop own strategies to solve a problem and articulate their solutions, all while engaging in rich, meaningful discussions. When students have the time and space to show their thinking, you have an opportunity to witness and grasp students' mathematical understanding and make sense of their (possible) levels of knowledge.

In lesson study, during the debriefing (the last part of this process), you analyze the data collected in the lesson. The lesson study team shares their observations and what they learned about the lesson based on student data. In the cases I will present in this chapter, teachers paid special attention to students' mistakes during the problem solving to identify gaps in understanding and why. When students make a mistake, you have the opportunity of detecting the underlying understanding being developed. A conceptual or procedural mistake could demonstrate gaps in understanding, and it could be identified through student work and/or explanations (Trueman, 2019). When mistakes occur, it is expected that you facilitate student discussions by questioning and supporting students to reflect and revise their solutions, thus furthering their mathematical thinking and understanding. Students could also make minor mistakes – computational, graphic or careless – which can be remedied when students become more fluent in using certain strategies, as well as when they learn to reflect back on their procedural steps to ensure accuracy (checking answers). Certainly, when an activity is student-led and we allow students to make, identify and discuss mistakes, they gain confidence and they will take more risks while solving a problem.

In the reminder of this chapter, I will share a case of lesson study in which teachers learned about the value of open-ended activities through examining student mistakes. Following general description of the lesson study context and how teachers learned in the context, I will present two specific examples of student mistakes and how teachers gained insight into student thinking by carefully analyzing the mistakes in these examples. As teachers made sense of student mistakes and reflected on instructional decisions they had made for the research lesson, they gained the new appreciation for inclusive teaching and student mistakes.

## Inclusive mathematical activity: context of the study

The mathematical activity illustrated in this paper is part of the research lesson focused on teaching mathematics for social justice. In the semester-long lesson study process, six teachers who taught Grades 1 and 2 students in Southern California collaborated to teach a multi-digit subtraction lesson (see Table 4.1).

The teachers were interested in addressing issues of social justice as a part of the lesson, and at the same time they wanted to incorporate an inclusive mathematics activity as a main part of the lesson. The inclusive activity is open ended in nature, allowing students to develop their own strategies to solve a problem. With an inclusive activity, students articulate their solutions and engage in rich meaningful discussions (contrasted with more traditional lessons in which teachers show mathematical procedures and students follow the steps).

A central topic of the lesson was "heroes", with which students analyzed unbalanced gender representations among their own heroes, since the teachers considered the topic relevant in addressing a social justice issue for the students in Grades 1 and 2 (the actual lesson plan is found in the Appendix). The activity started with the question, "What are the qualities that define your heroes/role models/people to look up to?" The teacher led the discussion and wrote the adjectives that students used to define their heroes. Then students were asked to pick somebody that "they look up to" and wrote the person's name on a sticky note. The responses were then sorted by another teacher by genders (male/female). The teacher prepared two cups of cubes for each small group of students, with yellow cubes representing female heroes and green cubes representing male heroes. Meanwhile, the first teacher asked the students, "Do you think we have more female or male heroes? Why?"

Students then moved into small groups and found out *which gender group had more heroes*, and *how many more*, by using their own solution strategies. After all groups had

*Table 4.1* Teacher demographic data; all names are pseudonyms

|   | Names | # of years taught | # of years with LS | Grades taught |
|---|---|---|---|---|
| 1 | Alyson | 12 | 4 | 2nd, 3rd, 5th |
| 2 | Laura | 4 | 0 | 1st, 2nd, 4th |
| 3 | Heather | 1 | 0 | 1st |
| 4 | Daniel | 5 | 2 | 2nd, 3rd, 4th |
| 5 | Cora | 7 | 0 | TK, K, 2nd, 4th |
| 6 | Kyle | 3 | 1 | 1st, 2nd |
| 7 | Diana | 8 | 4 | 1st, 2nd, 3rd |

found their answers, the class moved to a whole group discussion in which (1) each group shared their strategy, (2) the teacher sorted the posters around the classroom, (3) students gallery-walked and thought about why the solutions were sorted in that specific way, (4) the teacher facilitated student discussion about the similarities and differences about the strategies used and about why students thought there were more male or female heroes, and (5) students made connections to the characteristics of heroes discussed at the beginning of the lesson.

In the Grade 2 lesson, it was observed that all students (who worked in four groups) started their solutions by counting the cubes by tens to find the total of each group (39 and 48), but the strategies each group used to find the difference varied across them. The different groups used various strategies: three of them used Begin With One Number (BWON) strategies, and one group used the Decompose Tens and Ones (DTO) strategy (see the Appendix for a description of students' conceptions of multi-digit numbers and operations).

Students shared their strategies and discussed the mistakes that some of the groups made. After the gallery walk, students were able to identify the two major strategies used and the differences among them, emphasizing that some strategies were more abstract than others. Unfortunately, because of the lack of time, students didn't have the opportunity to deeply compare strategies, evaluate different approaches and find mathematical patterns.

## Teacher learning and understanding about the nature of the activity

One of the main ideas discussed during the debriefing was the nature of the activity. During the planning stages of lesson study, teachers created a mathematical task that was open ended, connected to something that students knew and could relate to. The teachers also decided to use a *blank paper*, so students had freedom to create, explore, represent and discuss their own solutions.

*Alyson:* Connecting it to things that they know then the numbers aren't just random numbers. They're numbers the kids are choosing somehow. And I like how open ended it was, a lot of possibilities, and we just need some chart paper and markers.

An open-ended task is a problem which has more than one correct answer or allows students to use more than one strategy to find the answer, in which students are expected to explain their answers and strategies. Furthermore, when teachers use tasks with language and context that connect to students' lived experiences, they are creating a space that supports the active engagement of all students, because all students have the opportunity to generate and share ideas. Teachers understood that this inclusive, open-ended activity could offer a differentiated instruction in which all students participate and engage in rich mathematical tasks, understanding that all students can show "great success in math". By providing different group settings and letting students lead the discussions, teachers could also see atypical group dynamics, where some "more quiet students" contributed and shared their ideas.

*Daniel:* It was kind of a differentiated lesson, in a sense that we opened it up to a problem that could be total or change unknown. You get different levels of math, and by giving everyone a chance to get something and find a solution, all worked on rich math.

*Kyle:* I was really proud because a lot of my really low readers were showing great success in the math. Like Jack, Nico and Sophia, like they're not my high-flying readers,

30  *Judith Fabrega*

but they understood the math problem enough to be able to tackle it and explain it. Well, look at Nico's explanation!

*Diana:* All the students were active, and we saw many different group dynamics. Different leaders would step up.

This lesson activity provided more equitable access to knowledge, as teachers proposed a task that "enabled all students to engage in challenging content, and they established and reinforced expectations for various ways to participate in and contribute to classroom activities" (Schoenfeld & the Teaching for Robust Understanding Project, 2016) (see Figures 4.1 and 4.2).

One of the aspects to improve in this lesson, according to the teachers, was to give more time for the whole group discussion.

*Kyle:* So we miss them [strategies]. We knew them because we were going around the tables, but the students were not able to listen to that. So I guess if I will have to teach that lesson again, I will definitely save more time to go deeply in those strategies. Because they were ALL great! I would start the discussion saying that some of the groups said the solution was 9 and some 8, so let's find why. And then each group shares deeply their strategy and they discuss about it.

The written lesson plan included the time for whole group discussion in which students will share and compare their strategies. However, because the small-group work took longer in the actual lesson, students could only present their strategies and solutions and discuss mistakes, but they didn't have the opportunity of comparing strategies to evaluate different

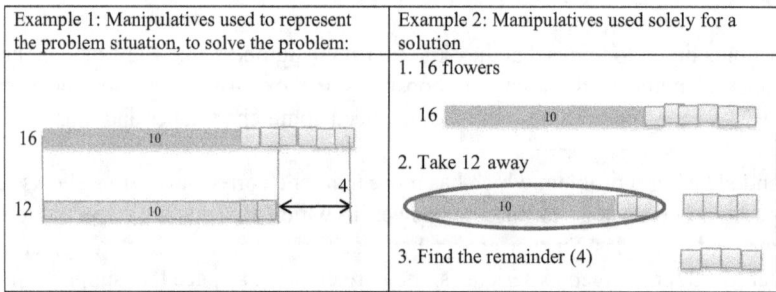

*Figure 4.1* Examples of manipulatives uses for 16 − 12 (e.g. "There are 16 red flowers and 12 white flowers. How many more red flowers are there?")

> Brainstorm an open-ended lesson activity for your grade level. Open-ended activity means the problem is presented without prescribed solution first, it is new to the students (they have never solved a problem like that before) while they can use what they have learned before to try to solve the problem, and it can be solved in multiple ways, by student attempting to use their prior knowledge. Think of different student solutions based on their prior knowledge. How would you facilitate their discussion given these solutions?

*Figure 4.2* Thinking box 1: open-ended lesson activity

approaches and find mathematical patterns. The goal of the whole group discussion should be to build on one another's solutions to develop mathematical ideas, not only to present solutions. It is essential, then, that you not only plan enough time for discussion but also plan how they are going to facilitate discussion. You can ask questions for students to articulate solution processes, compare different aspects of the strategies, and guide them to see connections among different strategies. Thus, the questions should focus on mathematical meaning and the relationship between mathematical ideas and representations, making the mathematics visible for all students.

In the following sections I will present two examples of students' strategies, the mistakes they made while solving the problem and the teacher learning that occurred during the debriefing when unpacking students' learning and understanding. As a reminder, students were working on finding the difference between two numbers: 39 and 48.

## Case one – Group 3: BWON strategy, coordinating the solution steps

In Group 3, the conversation started with one student's (Andrea) idea of adding 10 more to the "first number" (39) to make the difference 11 (didn't say why). Andrea knew she had changed the numbers by one (39 + 10 = 49; it is one more that she needed), and she knew she had to change the answer, too. However, instead of subtracting 1 from the 10 already added to the 39, she added it, making 11 her answer.

The group followed with the idea of finding a 10, adding 1 to 39. They wanted to use the decade number (40) as a reference number, as they knew that would make the solution more manageable.

$$39 + 1 = 40$$

After adding 1 to 39 to get 40, they knew they still had to do something else. One student said that they had to get to 48, so she suggested to "add something else to 40". Quickly, another student responded that they needed 8 to go to 48.

$$40 + 8 = 48$$

Although the process was correct, the students did not take one more necessary step to find the final answer. Students got 8 as their final answer because they forgot they had already added a 1 in the first step of the solution process (39 + 1), which would had made their final answer $8 + 1 = 9$.

In this group, students demonstrated that they could use place value to chunk numbers differently in problem solving. Andrea suggested to find a more "friendly number", which is a known strategy that students have learned in the past, and 40 was the first decade number they could find. Once they found the decade number, students could quickly find how many more they needed to go up to 48 (8) because of their place value knowledge (40 + 8 = 48). This group's solution process illustrates how challenging it can be to monitor different steps of subtraction problem solving. While every part of the solution process was well executed and reasonable, the students did not coordinate the two resulting quantities at the end (1 and 8) for the correct answer. Unlike addition problems, mistakes with subtraction problems often come from not coordinating the solution steps and monitoring different partial answers (Baroody, 1987; Baroody, Lai, & Mix, 2006)

## Supporting teacher learning: what did students' mistakes tell the teachers?

Careful examination of student discussions in small groups while they solve mathematics problems can provide you valuable information about students' mathematical thinking and understanding, creating pedagogically powerful moments in the classrooms. When you ask questions to push student thinking, students will also reflect on and become better aware of their processes, examine their mistakes, articulate solution paths and develop a better understanding of the strategies they use.

One major benefit that teachers in this study identified was that they were able to understand where some students' mistakes had come from, which they wouldn't have understood if students didn't have the time and space to discuss their own thinking during the problem-solving process. For example, Alyson was able to understand why one of the students thought that 11 could be the solution to the problem and the mathematical reasoning that helped the student arrive at that number:

*Alyson*: And they were counting by tens, so 39 to 49, but then they went the wrong way, like they would either pick 11 or 9, they knew it was a different 1, but they didn't know which way.

*Diana*: If they didn't understand the problem, at least I know where it comes from and what I'm doing now to fix that or to help them with that.

### Instructional implications

The student mistakes helped teachers reflect on how students were developing their understanding of numbers. For the first mistake, students added 1 to 10 instead of subtracting, and for the second mistake, they forgot to add the 1 from the beginning of the solution process to the final answer. Taking time to tease out the process and see why students thought in certain ways in the problem-solving process helped teachers gain better understanding of student thinking and appreciation for the mistakes.

For the first mistake, Andrea knew a relationship between the $9 + 1 = 10$ and the result that she was trying to obtain ($39 + 9 = 48$), but when using all the numbers together, she decided to add 1 to 10 instead of subtracting. Andrea is developing her understanding of 10 and of the relationship in between operations. She used a correct strategy, but the steps taken to execute that strategy were wrong. In this case, it would be beneficial to use questioning and discussion as an instructional tool to help her revise their thinking and problem-solving process. Questions such as "Does that answer make sense?" or "What are you trying to find in this question?" may help Andrea to reflect on her mathematical understanding.

For the second mistake, students made a minor error due to one number getting lost in the discussion. Students started the strategy by making a decade number (40), then continuing to discuss the solution process. By the end of the conversation, however, they forgot to see the entire solution process again and did not add the 1 they used to make the decade number at the beginning ($39 + 1$). In this case, students may just need assistance in checking the entire problem-solving process, keeping track of all the numbers they are coordinating through it, to make sure their work is accurate.

One of the most common mistakes students can make is focusing on the operation process and forgetting what the original question was, thus not getting the right answer. In this case, because there is probably not a conceptual or procedural mistake, you could support the student by reminding them to go back to the original problem situation and assisting them in developing strategies to check their work. Students may just need to go back through their own problem-solving process and revise every step, go back to the initial question, and check if their solution answers it and/or question if their answer makes sense (see Figure 4.3).

*Teacher learning through seeing mistakes* 33

> Think about a time when one of your students made a mistake which puzzled you. If possible, find the original work, of if you can remember, write out the process in which the mistake was made. Can you trace the student thinking process to explain why the mistake was made? As discussed in this chapter, some mistakes are simply technical and easy to fix, but there are other more-thoughtful mistakes essential in their learning. Explain how the student was learning by making the mistake.

*Figure 4.3* Thinking box 2: how students think through mistakes

## Case two – Group 4: DTO strategy, right answer but wrong use of the manipulatives

Unlike the rest of the groups, the students in Group 4 did not start with one number and find the distance to the second. Instead they started with breaking apart the two numbers by place value. According to the teacher, they had recently been using "number bonds" to break apart numbers to solve addition problems, and perhaps that was the reason why students started breaking the numbers apart, although they had barely discussed the question and what they needed to find out.

Once the numbers were decomposed, students discussed subtracting 40 – 30 (numbers on the tens place), and 8–9 (numbers on the ones place), but they got stuck in this step. David quickly found the difference between 40 and 30, and without writing it down, he shared with the rest of the group that the first difference was 10. However, then he started a sentence with "8 minus 9" and kept thinking, but he never finished the sentence. The rest of the students didn't follow the idea, and they moved on to using cubes to represent the problem. It is important to notice that no one suggested 9 – 8, which would be a common error for students using this method, demonstrating their knowledge of the subtraction process, taking the smaller number away from the bigger number.

Then, students decided to use the cubes on the table as they talked:

Liam: We can take out three green groups [groups of 10] and three yellow groups.
Julia: How many do we have here [green]?
Andrew: We have more greens.
Liam: [Moving cubes one by one using the nine yellows and starting by the eight greens outside of the group] One, two, three, four, five, six, seven, eight, nine.

Once they moved all the cubes, students figured out they had nine green cubes left. However, they never went back to the equation to translate in numbers how to decompose one of the tens in 48 to be able to subtract 39. Students used cubes as a tool, but theirs was not the most appropriate use for subtraction. Unlike addition, the cubes cannot represent both minuend and subtrahend in the solution process, because the subtrahend (39) is a part of the minuend (48). When solving a comparison subtraction problem, representation of the problem situation becomes crucial before students engage in the subtraction solution process. In terms of this particular problem situation, it is appropriate to provide students with two sets of cubes, representing the two quantities in the problem. When two sets of cubes are provided to represent two quantities, students would naturally represent the problem situation first and then solve it by comparing both sets of cubes (see Figure 4.1, example 1). With enough experiences and exposures to different subtraction problems, students would gradually come to generalize all types of subtraction problems more abstractly, and they would use the cubes solely to model a solution strategy over time (see Figure 4.1, example 2). It is important for you to know this student learning trajectory and thus guide their attention to the difference represented by only one group of cubes in Example 2.

Using manipulatives allowed the students to figure out a solution in a way they could not figure out by breaking apart numbers on the paper. They still decomposed tens and ones because when using the cubes, they figured out that in order to subtract nine yellow cubes (matching green cubes with yellow cubes), they needed to break apart one group of ten green cubes and use one of them. Thus, students were able to understand that they needed to regroup the cubes to solve the problem. Instead of *4 tens 8 ones*, students worked with *3 tens and 18 ones* green cubes which allow them to match and subtract *3 tens and 9 ones* yellow cubes. This method helps students to understand the standard algorithm by allowing them to visualize how place value works in subtraction problems.

### *Supporting teacher learning: what did students' mistakes tell the teachers?*

During debriefing, teachers talked about the materials and manipulatives that they offered to the students to support the invention of mathematical strategies. Manipulatives are a great tool to help make student thinking visible and concrete, making it possible for students to resolve misconceptions and/or (in this particular problem) reinforce place value in mathematical thinking. However, teachers didn't discuss how Group 4 used the manipulatives and possible ways the teachers could have supported more abstract thinking.

*Caitlin*: Even the number line, the students were literally placing the cubes on top of the number line and I don't know, the material that we put at the table may shape the strategies that they use, but also give them more opportunities. Because if they didn't have any material, then my guess is that I don't know, maybe they will use whatever we did more recently, or even the standard algorithm.

*Katie*: I need to start using all those manipulatives. I need to put out some of the tools. Yeah, I know it might actually don't naturally go grab them, but it will help.

### *Instructional implications*

One important aspect to consider when solving multi-digit subtraction problems is the tools that students have access to. For subtraction, it is important to use the tools (e.g. manipulatives) to represent the problem situation accurately. There are different kinds of subtraction problems, and in particular, comparison problems such as the one used in the study naturally invite students to represent two different quantities (minuend and subtrahend) to compare. While it is appropriate to do so in representing the problem situation, that can ultimately generate confusion in solving the problem. For a solution, it is better if students represent the minuend concretely and take the quantity of subtrahend away from the minuend. This requires practices for students to move from representing the problem context purely for its context to representing it for problem-solving purposes. For other kinds of subtraction problems

> Why do you think open-ended lesson activities are necessary for students to show different ways of thinking? Why a more-traditional problem-solving, where a teacher models the solution, is less likely to invite students to think creatively? Do you think it's better for students to learn one correct solution method and not experiencing different ways of thinking so that they won't get confused? Discuss the value of open-ended lesson activities in your group.

*Figure 4.4* Thinking box 3: the relationship between open-ended activity, multiple student solutions and learning from making mistakes

(e.g. change problems, part-part-whole problems), representing the minuend at the beginning of the problem-solving process comes naturally, and students are likely to be able to work with one quantity. The challenge discussed here only applies to comparison problems.

Another important aspect of student learning illustrated in the study is about base-ten place value understanding. In this particular case, it would help students understand how to break apart a 10 in ten 1s, regroup the given quantities differently and subtract numbers as required in the problem to find the answer. Students would also learn how regrouping of quantities would translate in equation form. The manipulatives can facilitate understanding of the concept as students regroup quantities across places, and you can also help students make connections with how the representation and the steps of the algorithm work, along with concrete manipulation of manipulatives, so that students can think more abstractly about the problem situation and learn to use more formal methods (see Figure 4.4).

## Conclusions

Lesson study is a perfect setting to reconsider what mistakes are and how to use them to make sense of student thinking and possible partial understanding of students. In order to surface such understanding in the lesson, open-ended activities are essential, and we want to make sure the problems we choose for our research lessons are open enough. It would not only create an opportunity for you to witness and grasp students' mathematical understanding and make sense of where meaningful mistakes came from, but it would also help you realize how open-ended activities support the active participation of all students and provide a setting to engage in rich mathematical tasks.

Often teachers do not pay attention to students' mistakes, merely dismissing them as indicators that students didn't understand a concept, or simply treating errors as something that "just needs to be fixed". While avoiding and ignoring mistakes appears to be common in the classroom, students would actually benefit from making, identifying and discussing certain mistakes. Teachers in this study gained appreciation for students' mistakes as a window into their thinking. As the two cases illustrate, when you pay close attention to students' mistakes, you will able to identify the origin of students' partial understanding and how they are thinking. This process may help you to analyze which changes need to be made in the lesson to meet students' needs and help them move forward.

There is also a very clear benefit for students when instruction is based on collaborative and inclusive activities. First, small-group settings bring more student-led discussions, allow students to see different approaches to solving problems and, as seen in this study, students feel more confident to participate and contribute in the problem-solving process. Moreover, when you focus on the process instead of the result and treat mistakes as an opportunity for learning, it takes off the pressure of "being right" from the students. This will translate in more confident students who feel safe to take risks and explore a variety of paths to solve a problem.

In lesson study, expand your discussion beyond lesson steps, discuss common mistakes students make or typical challenges they experience with the lesson topics and focus on both correct and incorrect strategies. Our instruction needs to move beyond focusing only on correct procedures and right answers to how to facilitate student discussions of variety of strategies, correct and incorrect, so that students can explore and learn more mathematics together.

## Acknowledgement to teachers and students

This chapter would have not been possible without the amazing teachers who were part of the lesson study team. They share their expertise and use their experience to create this mathematical activity. We also thank all the students who were really engaged in the solution of the problem and welcomed all of us into their classrooms.

## Additional readings

Barlow, A., Duncan, M., Lischka, A., Hartland, K., & Willingham, J. (2017, May). Are your students problem performers or problem solvers? *Teaching Children Mathematics, 23*, 550–558.

Baroody, A. J. (1987). *Children's mathematical thinking: A developmental framework for preschool, primary, and special education teachers*. New York, NY: Teachers College Press.

Baroody, A. J., Lai, M., & Mix, K. S. (2006). The development of young children's early number and operation sense and its implications for early childhood education. *Handbook of Research on the Education of Young Children, 2*, 187–221.

Bray, W. (2013). How to leverage the potential of mathematical errors. *Teaching Children Mathematics, 19*, 424–431.

Carpenter, T. P., Franke, M. L., Jacobs, V. R., Fennema, E., & Empson, S. B. (1998). A longitudinal study of invention and understanding in children's multidigit addition and subtraction. *Journal for Research in Mathematics Education, 29*(1), 3. https://doi.org/10.2307/749715

Carpenter, T. P., & Moser, J. M. (1984). The acquisition of addition and subtraction concepts in grades one through three. *Journal for Research in Mathematics Education, 15*(3), 179. https://doi.org/10.2307/748348

Fuson, K. C. (1992). Research on whole number addition and subtraction. In *Handbook of research on mathematics teaching and learning: A project of the National Council of Teachers of Mathematics* (pp. 243–275). New York, NY: Macmillan.

Gojak, L. (2013). *The power of a good mistake*. NCTM Summing Up. Retrieved from https://www.nctm.org/News-and-Calendar/Messages-from-the-President/Archive/Linda-M_-Gojak/The-Power-of-a-Good-Mistake/

Murata, A. (2004). Paths to learning ten-structured understandings of teen sums: Addition solution methods of Japanese grade 1 students. *Cognition and Instruction, 22*(2), 185–218. https://doi.org/10.1207/s1532690xci2202_2

Murata, A., & Fuson, K. C. (2006). Teaching as assisting individual constructive paths within an interdependent class learning zone: Japanese first graders learning to add using 10. *Journal for Research in Mathematics Education, 37*(5), 421–456.

Murata, A., & Stewart, C. (2017). Facilitating mathematical practices through visual representations. *Teaching Children Mathematics, 23*(7), 404–412.

Schoenfeld, A. H., & the Teaching for Robust Understanding Project. (2016a). *The Teaching for Robust Understanding (TRU) observation guide: A tool for teachers, coaches, administrators, and professional learning communities*. Berkeley, CA: Graduate School of Education, University of California, Berkeley. Retrieved from http://map.mathshell.org/

Trueman. (2019). What That Mistake Tells You. *Teaching Children Mathematics, 25*(6), 380. https://doi.org/10.5951/teacchilmath.25.6.0380

# Appendix
## Students' conceptions of multi-digit numbers and operations

Considering three quantities involved in the subtraction number relationships (0 − 0 = 0), children may use three different levels of conception of quantities to solve the subtraction problem (Table 4.2).

When it comes to multi-digit operations, students may use two general methods: (1) the Decompose Tens and Ones (DTO) method and (2) the Begin With One Number (BWON) method. For the DTO method, students split the numbers by place value and operate them individually by places (e.g. for 69 − 32, decompose 69 into 60 and 9, 32 into 30 and 2, subtract tens 60 − 30 = 30, then ones 9 − 2 = 7, then add them together 30 + 7 = 37). For the BWON method, students start with the minuend and make sequential moves by the chunks of the subtrahend (e.g. for 58 − 21, 58 − 20 = 38, then 38 − 1 = 37). Students may also combine some parts of these two approaches to find answers.

Students' strategies require complex, multiple steps that need to be coordinated, and these steps reflect students' thinking process. The DTO strategy takes advantage of students' understanding of place value, supporting learning for their future use of the common algorithm. The DTO method is important in students' future learning of multi-digit subtraction and place-value concept, because it makes a foundation for students' 10-based multi-digit

*Table 4.2* Levels of conception of quantities

| | |
|---|---|
| **Level I: Count-all-and-take-away strategy**<br>Children consider all quantities as collections of individual units. When taking a part of a set, children count each individual set one at a time. | For 9 − 5, children would count 9 unitarily "1, 2, 3, 4, 5, 6, 7, 8, 9", then count 5 "1, 2, 3, 4, 5, 6, 7, 8, 9", and finally count the rest starting from 1. |
| **Level II: Count-down or count-up strategy**<br>Children abbreviate the subtrahend or the minuend to find the difference. | Count-down: For 13 − 2, children will start with the minuend (13) and count back two times to figure out the difference, "13 . . . 12, 11" to get an answer of 11.<br><br>Count up: For 10 − 7, students will start with the subtrahend (7) and count up to the minuend, "7 . . . 8, 9, 10" to get a difference of 3. |
| **Level III: Ideal chunking numbers strategy**<br>At the final level, children understand how different numbers relate to one another and find the difference using the knowledge of number relations. | Understand that 3 and 3 make 6, thus 7 − 3 must be 4, because 7 is 1 more than 6. |

thinking by requiring them to chunk 10s (Murata, 2004). The BWON strategy, in contrast, shows how students consider numbers in chunks, whether using place value thinking or not, while also using the relational understanding among different quantities in the problem. By focusing on how students coordinate different steps and uniquely manipulate numbers through the problem-solving processes, we get a glimpse of their mathematical thinking and developing number sense.

# 5 Going deeper into lesson study through *kyouzai kenkyuu*

*Ban Heng Choy and Christine Kim-Eng Lee*

## *Kyouzai kenkyuu*: an often neglected aspect of lesson study

*Kyouzai kenkyuu*, or the "study of materials for teaching", is a critical yet often neglected phase in lesson study adopted in countries beyond Japan, although it is very much a part of daily practice of Japanese teachers. This curriculum study phase allows teachers to carefully examine curriculum documents, textbooks, teaching and learning materials, and subject matter and read relevant research to inform the development of a unit within which is embedded the research lesson. One reason why teachers "often fail to conduct lesson study in a way that sufficiently impacts their pedagogical content knowledge is the failure to engage adequately in *kyouzai kenkyuu*" (Yoshida & Jackson, 2011). Given its importance, it is crucial for teachers to understand the essence of *kyouzai kenkyuu* and conduct this phase of lesson study beyond a superficial level. In this chapter, we will explain the main inquiry processes involved in *kyouzai kenkyuu*, provide some guidelines for lesson study practitioners, and illustrate these ideas using two snapshots of practice from our work with teachers.

## What is *kyouzai kenkyuu*?

> Teachers can provide the richness of learning experiences for students in the classroom only up to the level of their understanding of the instructional materials, so it is important for the teachers to carry out *kyouzai kenkyuu* every day through classroom practice.

The preceding quote is what Japanese teachers say about *kyouzai kenkyuu* (Yoshida, 2011). It is part and parcel of their daily practice and integral to the culture of Japanese teaching. The literal translation of *kyouzai kenkyuu* refers to the study (as in *kenkyuu*) of instructional (as in *kyo*) materials (as in *zai*) (Watanabe et al., 2008). But what do we mean by the study of instructional materials? Does it refer to the study of textbooks? It is true that textbooks play a central role in schooling for both teachers and students. Studying textbooks will be an important part of the *kyouzai kenkyuu* process. However, studying textbooks does not mean reading through them to understand the content. Rather, it requires teachers to examine the flow of the content and how ideas are connected to each other within and across topics. Many lesson study practitioners will agree that *kyouzai kenkyuu* is an important part of lesson study, but what it means is not well captured by the literal translation of the term.

> **Key idea**
>
> The practice of *kyouzai kenkyuu* is not captured well by the direct translation – "instructional materials research" – as it is lacking in meaning and depth of what Japanese educators do during *kyouzai kenkyuu*. Just like other cultural practice, the name is not enough to capture a deep understanding of the practice (Melville, 2017, p. 3).

*Kyouzai kenkyuu* is certainly more than studying textbooks, and it may be productive to think of the process as a form of research. Yokosuka (1990) as cited in Watanabe et al. (2008) defined *kyouzai kenkyuu* as

> the entire process of research activities related to *kyouzai*, beginning with the selection/development, deepening the understanding of the true nature of a particular *kyouzai*, planning a lesson with a particular *kyouzai* that matches the current state of the students, culminating in the development of an instructional plan.
>
> (Yokosuka, 1990, p. 73)

Here, the emphasis of *kyouzai kenkyuu* is to study the "*kyouzai* from a child's perspective, or an attempt to look at *kyouzai* as children would and anticipate their responses and reactions to *kyouzai*" (Yoshida, 1999). In other words, teachers investigate the instructional materials by examining students' thinking, understanding and learning. This process generates ideas for improving instructional materials, student learning and teaching. This way, teachers not only understand the instructional materials from their own perspectives but also see the content from their students' perspectives.

To this end, Watanabe et al. (2008) described two types of *kyouzai kenkyuu*, as explained in a Japanese dictionary. First, teachers study materials that were already developed (textbooks, teacher manuals, student workbooks) deeply and repeatedly to understand the nature of the instructional materials and assess whether the materials are suitable for their classrooms. Second, teachers investigate in-depth the particular subject matter to be taught. In so doing, teachers investigate the relationship between the readily available instructional materials and the subject matter to be taught and how students can be brought to understand the subject matter of the lessons. The teachers develop a clear vision of what they want to teach (or what they want students to understand) using the instructional materials, and that vision provides the foundation of the lesson.

The question, then, is not merely how to use the textbooks/instructional materials but how to teach *students* the subject matter with the textbooks/instructional materials. Answering this question will require a careful analysis of the topic in accordance with the objective(s) of the lesson (Shimizu, 1999). The process includes analyses of the connections both among the current and previous topics (and forthcoming ones, in some cases) and within the topic itself. In addition, *kyouzai kenkyuu* will involve a deliberate anticipation of students' approaches to the problem tasks used in the lesson and the planning of instructional activities based on these anticipated responses. To sum up, Shimizu's description positions *kyouzai kenkyuu* as being more than a study of instructional materials. In essence, *kyouzai kenkyuu* is a student-centric process which involves an anticipation of students' approaches to the problem tasks selected or adapted for the lesson, an examination of students' thinking in relation to the topic, and the design of instructional activities to use in response to students' thinking.

## A snapshot of primary science teachers engaging in *kyouzai kenkyuu*

In this section, we will illustrate the key processes of *kyouzai kenkyuu* by examining how a group of primary science teachers in Singapore engaged in the process. During *kyouzai kenkyuu*, the teachers first deliberated on the research theme for their science lesson study and asked themselves what should be the potential goals for the learning of science for the students in their school. They drew reference from the student outcomes documented in the Ministry of Education's (MOE) primary science syllabus (MOE, 2014):

> The science curriculum seeks to nurture the student as an inquirer. The starting point is that children are curious about and want to explore the things around them. The science curriculum leverages on and seeks to fuel this spirit of curiosity. The end goal is students who enjoy science and value science as an important tool in helping them explore their natural and physical world.

By examining the gap between the actual and ideal profiles of science students they would like to achieve, the teachers decided on the following as their research theme: "If we make Science relevant to the daily lives of our children and provide opportunities for them to work together, this will spark curiosity in our children to ask questions and share their thinking with one another". This theme drove the planning of the unit on the topic of light, within which is embedded the research lesson plan. The teachers examined the national syllabus for primary science, the scope and sequence of the unit of work on light and the links between units. As active curriculum makers, they asked what, why and who are they teaching, and how can their students be taught in ways to ignite curiosity in science. The key and linking questions shown in Table 5.1 form the framework of the content of the unit on the topic of light.

The teachers explored the students' misconceptions and lack of understanding of the concept of light from a diagnostic test and analysis of past years' students' assessments. They found that some of the students did not have an understanding of the scientific explanation

*Table 5.1* Framework of the content of the unit on "light"

| Lesson | Linking questions | Key ideas | Pedagogical principles of 5Es in scientific inquiry |
|---|---|---|---|
| 1 | What are the sources of light? | There are different sources of light. | Engage |
| 2 | Why can we see objects? | We can see objects because they reflect light or are sources of light. | Explore/Explain |
| 3 | How does light travel? | Light travels in a straight line. | Explore/Explain |
| 4 | Do all objects allow light to pass through? | The amount of light passing through an object depends on the transparency of the material of that object. | Explain |
| 5 | What happens when light cannot pass through an object? | A shadow is formed when light is completely or partially blocked by an object. | Elaborate |
| 6 | What will we see when light shines on an object? | It is possible to describe what we will see when light interacts with objects and materials. | Evaluate |

of vision. The students were not aware that they were able to see an object when it was a source of light (e.g. a lit candle) or when it reflected light. There were a lot of misconceptions about shadows. The students did not perceive that the source of light was always on the opposite side of the object to the shadow and drew the shadow in the wrong direction. They perceived that a shadow was detached from the object and had details. They drew a shadow not as a solid area and drew a wrong shape for the shadow. They did not know the difference between a reflection and a shadow. The students wrongly identified the moon as a source of light. They also perceived shiny objects as sources of light. The teachers were also concerned that their students were not aware that light travels in straight lines and that light could be reflected.

This *kyouzai kenkyuu* phase of the teachers' collaborative discussions pushed the teachers to think more deeply about the content of the unit on light they were teaching. It led to the uncovering of their own understanding of the subject matter of light. According to Yoshida and Jackson (2011), "what a teacher knows is one of the most important influences on what teachers can do in the classroom to support students' learning" (p. 280). They were challenged in their usual practice of dependence on MOE curriculum framework, materials and workbooks, and they designed their own activities to make science authentic and relevant to the daily lives of their children and to deal with students' misconceptions. They read literature to learn more about the topic and how to teach it in ways that are relevant to the daily lives of the children and how to design learning activities that are authentic and hands-on.

---

**Thinking point 1**

From the descriptions provided in the practice of Japanese teachers and a case in Singapore:

- What do you see as the different facets of *kyouzai kenkyuu*?
- Which facet do you find most challenging to do, and why?
- How can you look at kyouzai from a child's perspective?
- How can *kyouzai kenkyuu* be part of your daily practice?

---

## Improving *kyouzai kenkyuu*: what can teachers do?

Few people will argue against the importance of conducting detailed *kyouzai kenkyuu*. However, teachers often see lesson study as lesson planning and not as curriculum making and are short-sighted in their focus of only planning research lessons for observations (Lim, Lee, Saito, & Syed Haron, 2011). They go through the mechanics of lesson study protocols with inadequate attention paid to *kyouzai kenkyuu*. Moreover, it is not trivial for teachers to engage productively in *kyouzai kenkyuu* (Lee & Choy, 2017), and the process is intensive and complex (Yoshida, 1999). So, what can teachers do to improve their *kyouzai kenkyuu*? In this section, we will highlight three ideas for lesson study practitioners to consider.

### *Use key guiding questions*

First, it is crucial to understand that the inquiry process in *kyouzai kenkyuu* is the key to learning from the process of lesson study. Through the inquiry in *kyouzai kenkyuu*, teachers develop a unit plan, establish clear and focused learning goals and student outcomes, decide use of instructional tools, anticipate student responses and provide support, and consider critical areas for teachers to observe during live observation of the research lesson (Yoshida, 2011). One way to do this is through the use of guiding questions. The questions teachers asked during the inquiry of the materials and subject matter positioned them as thoughtful professionals and as curriculum makers for enactment in the classroom. You will notice that the science teachers in the case described earlier in this chapter used some of the following inquiry questions during the *kyouzai kenkyuu* phase of the lesson study cycle.

---

**Questions to guide inquiry during *kyouzai kenkyuu***

**Why are we teaching this topic?**

1. Why do my students need to learn this topic? (Identification of goals and reference made to national/state standards, if any.)
2. What is/are the reason(s) for teaching this idea at this particular point in the curriculum? (Rationale for teaching the topic and its place in the scope and sequence of a unit.)

**What are we teaching?**

3. What do my students need to know and understand?
4. What do these ideas really mean? How do these ideas relate to one another? (Coherence of key ideas within a lesson.)

**Who are we teaching?**

5. What ideas do students already understand that can be used as a starting point for this new idea? (Use of prior knowledge.)
6. What misconceptions do my students have about the various ideas in the topic? (Misconceptions and diagnosis of students' understanding prior to learning the topic.)

**How do we teach so that students will learn?**

7. Why is this particular problem or activity useful in helping students develop this new idea? (Design of task/learning activity and selection of problems.)
8. How can students solve this problem using what they already know, and how can their solution strategies be used to develop this new idea? (Using prior knowledge for problem solving and development of new ideas.)
9. What are the common mistakes? Why do students make such mistakes? How should teachers respond to these mistakes? (Students' misconceptions as they arise in their learning.)
10. What manipulatives and other materials should be provided to students? How do they influence students' learning? (Selection of instructional materials and resources.)

**How can we plan for transfer of learning?**

11. What new ideas are students expected to build using this idea in the future? (Transfer of learning/application.)

*Table 5.2* Description of the three-point framework

| Three-point framework (Yang & Ricks, 2012)/ Choy's (2016) 3C questions | Description |
| --- | --- |
| Key point (concept) | This refers to the key ideas or big ideas of the lesson. By considering the key point of the lesson, teachers can begin to unpack the idea into its associated concepts, conventions, results, techniques and mathematical processes. |
| Difficult point (confusion) | Here we consider students' confusion or stumbling blocks that make the learning of the key idea difficult. By understanding what makes students confused and why they are confused, teachers can begin to think about possible approaches to teaching. |
| Critical point (course of action) | Thinking about students' confusion leads teachers to think about possible courses of action to address the difficulty. It is important for teachers to examine whether the course of action addresses the difficulty students have and how the course of action could smoothen the learning process. |

Besides using these specific questions, it is sometimes useful to realize that these questions can also be classified into three main categories: those related to content, those related to students' learning and those related to teachers' pedagogy. As such, it may also be good for teachers to use Yang and Ricks's (2012) three-point framework (the key point, difficult point, and critical point) or an adaptation of the three-point framework by Choy (2016) to guide the inquiry process by considering the alignment between the concept, confusion and course of action as described in Table 5.2.

## *Use good curriculum materials*

Yoshida (2011) suggested that *kyouzai kenkyuu* can be enhanced with "the best available curricular materials that are grounded in strong content and pedagogical knowledge" as well as "coherent and focused curriculum". For a start, teachers should access the various subject syllabi or curriculum standards, teacher guides and other instructional materials produced by their respective departments or ministries of education and other professional organizations which they could use for *kyouzai kenkyuu*. For instance, teachers in Singapore could refer to the *Teaching and Learning Guides* produced by the ministry for the different subjects. In the United States, teachers could look for instructional materials from the National Science Teachers Association (NSTA), the National Council of Teachers of Mathematics (NCTM) and even museums such as the Smithsonian or the California Academy of Sciences, to name a few. Elsewhere in the world, teachers can also refer to best practice materials produced by international organizations such as the Organisation for Economic Co-operation and Development (OECD) and the International Bureau of Education at UNESCO (e.g. the Educational Practices Series at www.ibe.unesco.org/en/resources/educational-practices).

Teachers can refer to textbooks and curriculum guides published in countries other than their own. For example, Japanese math textbooks are now published in English (e.g. Tokyo Shoseki's *Mathematics International* [Grades 7–9] textbooks). These are the most widely used lower secondary school mathematics textbooks in Japan. Japanese teachers use these textbooks to develop dynamic lessons using a structured problem-solving approach (teaching through problem solving) to enhance the mathematical thinking and conceptual understanding of students. Studying these textbooks together with Tokyo Shoseki's *Mathematics International* (Grades 1–6) will help teachers and researchers see the big picture of how students in Japan are taught and how their understanding of mathematical concepts is developed. These are available from global education resources. Besides these international textbook resources, it may be helpful for teachers to examine how the different textbooks in their own countries develop the concepts and, at times, look at how the same topic is developed at the higher levels of education.

---

**Thinking point 2**

- What curriculum materials can you use to support your study of the curriculum of the topic you will be teaching?
- What useful research literature have you found about effective ways of teaching the topic?
- What misconceptions do your students have about the topic?
- How can you find out your students' misconceptions?
- What kinds of responses are your students likely to give to your questions as well as to the kinds of activities you have designed?
- How do you assess students' learning?

---

*Involve a knowledgeable other*

*Kyouzai kenkyuu* can be enhanced through the support of knowledgeable others, external resource persons and critical commentators. In Japan, retired school principals, university professors, subject association members, school superintendents and other professionals play the role of knowledgeable others. This is integral to lesson study practice in Japan not found in other countries. Many university professors visit schools to observe lessons several times within a week. In Fukui, faculty from the Department of the Professional Development of Teachers (DPDT) are housed in their attached schools and are available as co-curriculum designers as well as co-researchers with the teachers. There is a need to tap and develop such a resource in other countries beyond Japan by involving them in lesson study cycles in schools. Often, the knowledgeable other is involved only in observing the research lesson and final lesson commentary. However, it may also be useful to engage the knowledgeable other during the *kyouzai kenkyuu* phase so that teachers can tap his/her expertise to uncover learning points that would otherwise be missed by the teachers (Jiang, Choy, & Lee, 2019). In our research, we found the knowledgeable other pushing teachers to think more deeply about students' misconceptions and the flow of the key ideas within the topic to be taught. They helped teachers clarify their use of language with the children, rethink their design of learning activities, and challenge their reliance on one source of curriculum materials and their assumptions about what and why they are teaching the way they do (Lee, 2019).

> **Thinking point 3**
> - Who in your context can you involve as knowledgeable others?
> - How can you get buy-in from potential knowledgeable others to be involved in lesson study?
> - What kinds of training and development activities would you provide to your knowledgeable others?

## Snapshot of *kyouzai kenkyuu*: an example from a Singapore classroom

In this section, we illustrate some of the proposed guidelines using a second snapshot of *kyouzai kenkyuu* from our work with teachers (Choy, 2015). Our objective is not to highlight the opportunities missed by the teachers in their *kyouzai kenkyuu*. But rather, we want to highlight the opportunities offered by our proposed guidelines that might have added value to the teachers' discussion.

### Snapshot: a discussion on the gradient of straight-line graphs

*Use of guiding questions and good instructional materials*

> **Context of the snapshot**
>
> The vignettes described in this snapshot centred about the pedagogical reasoning and actions of Anita, a mathematics teacher with twelve years of teaching experience. Here, she planned a lesson on gradient with five other teachers from Springside Secondary School (Eddie, Winston, Teresa, Don and Kent) and taught the research lesson for Secondary One (aged 13) students. Eddie is the head of department. The researcher is not the knowledgeable other, but rather he was there more as an observer. The discussion described here occurred during the first session, in which Anita provided the first draft of the task, which took the form of a worksheet on finding gradients.

The teachers involved were introduced to Choy's adapted version of the three-point framework (see Table 5.2). As a result, the teachers were able to identify clearly the concept and the potential student confusion. Specifically, Anita identified the notion of gradient as "rise over run" for the lesson, and she highlighted that her students might have difficulties when the coordinate axes were introduced. Anita was very specific about students' errors and was able to provide possible examples of them. For instance, Anita highlighted that students might determine the "run" wrongly by taking reference to the origin (see Figure 5.1).

This episode highlights the usefulness of guiding questions to frame the discussion. The use of the adapted three-point framework provides a focal point for the teachers during their discussion. As demonstrated by Anita, it is better to be specific and elaborate on the three points using specific examples, rather than making vague comments which may not be useful. However, besides specificity, it is also important for the teachers to consider whether the

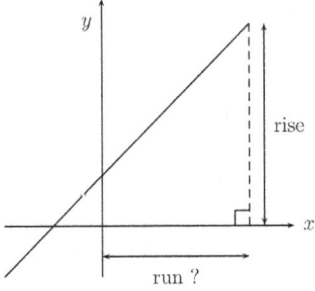

*Figure 5.1* A possible student error of calculating "run"

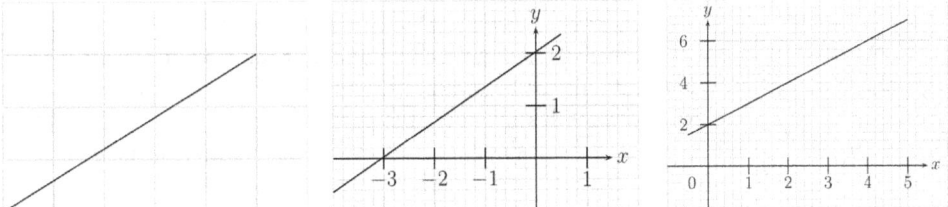

*Figure 5.2* Different types of questions in the worksheet

proposed course of action helps address the issue identified. For example, in this discussion, although Anita had a relatively strong grasp of the content and possible student errors, her comprehension did not necessarily transform into the design of her worksheet.

Referring to Figure 5.2, Anita used three types of questions in her worksheet: four questions on gradients of lines set in unmarked gridlines (Type A), six questions that involved the use of the standard Cartesian coordinates (Type B) and six questions which were situated in a non-homogeneous coordinate system (Type C). In each of the three types of questions, what counts as distance is different, and this may pose problems for students trying to find the "rise" and "run", especially when they are learning about coordinate systems for the first time. With a change of scale, distances are not preserved, and thus students may be confused about what to use for the rise and run. The selection of the questions suggests that Anita could have overlooked students' possible confusion about the effect of scale on distances.

Therefore, it is useful to keep in mind the following two things when using guiding questions:

1 Be specific. Give details and examples where relevant.
2 Discuss the alignment between the proposed course of action in relation to the students' confusion associated with the concept of the lesson.

In addition, this episode also highlights the need to consider the curriculum or instructional materials used. If Anita had looked at how the textbooks developed the topic, she would have noticed that the use of the coordinates was not explicitly taught in the textbook she was using and all the questions in the textbooks did not involve a change of scale.

*Include a knowledgeable other*

One issue that may arise during discussion is the lack of expert knowledge to point out the teachers' "blind spots". This may occur when teachers trivialize the difficulty of students. As seen from the following episode, Anita trivialized students' errors when Eddie asked whether her students could see the "rise" and "run".

| 1 | Eddie: | So, can they see? Can they see the rise over run? [He laughs.] So . . . we want to make sure that . . . |
|---|---|---|
| 2 | Anita: | Can see one. . . . I don't think they cannot see. . . . It's [obvious]. Can see . . . |
| 3 | Eddie: | So, the students know that for the "rise", they know how to count the squares? |
| 4 | Researcher: | Is this the first time they encounter this? |
| 5 | Anita: | Yeah. This is the first time. They are Secondary One [students]. |
| 6 | Eddie: | So, do they know this one? [Points to the formula "rise over run".] |
| 7 | Anita: | Sorry, I have been doing this for a long time already. At the beginning, the teacher will tell them that gradient is the measure of steepness or slope, so they will know that gradient is rise over run . . . then tell them that to measure the slope, it's rise over run. Just start with [calculating gradient]. |
| 8 | Researcher: | So, you define for them? |
| 9 | Anita: | Yes. Just tell them. It's just as simple as that. Gradient is just "rise over run". Some students, the better ones, can even tell you if they read the textbooks. |
| . . . | . . . | . . . |
| 14 | Eddie: | So, the rise is referring to . . . ? Let's say I am a student. What is rise? |
| 15 | Anita: | Eddie, this one they will have no problems. . . . I can tell you they know. [Eddie laughs.] They know that rise is the straight one [perpendicular]. This is not a problem to lower secondary students. |

Anita seemed confident that students could understand gradient simply by telling them (lines 7 and 9), and she expected them to see "rise" and "run" the same way she did. Eddie tried to get Anita see the possibility that this might not be the case by adopting the perspective of a student (line 14). Following the cue by Eddie (lines 14 and 16), the researcher in this case study, who is *not* the knowledgeable other, tried to probe Anita's thinking about "rise and run":

| 16 | Eddie: | So, what is rise? What is run? |
|---|---|---|
| 17 | Anita: | The height is the rise, then the run . . . |
| 18 | Researcher: | The height from where? |
| 19 | Anita: | The height from the bottom to the top of the mountain . . . |
| 20 | Researcher: | So, where's the bottom? So, for this line [points to a line on the worksheet], where is the bottom? |
| 21 | Anita: | Perpendicular? I mean, usually when I teach this topic, I will tell them that it is the line perpendicular to the straight line. I do not think they have a problem with that. I only intend to spend two to three minutes on this. I will tell them, during the introduction, that the bottom is the perpendicular line to the height. |

| 22 | Researcher: | So, where's the base for this line? |
|---|---|---|
| 23 | Anita: | The base is where the person is standing . . . [Points to the boy in Figure 5.2 Type A] |
| 24 | Researcher: | [Points to the left hand corner of the boy] So, is the base here? |
| 25 | Anita: | I trivialize all these because so far, I have not seen any of my students having problems counting the rise and the run. |

Here Anita focused on using explanations to help students overcome their confusion about the distances. She also asserted that she had not seen anyone having problems with "counting rise and run" (line 25). However, if an *external knowledgeable other* (not the researcher in this case) was engaged in the same discussion, it would have been easier for him/her to highlight that Anita's point contradicted the difficulty she had earlier identified (see Figure 5.2). In addition, the knowledgeable other could have pointed out that Anita's method of using the figure of a boy to indicate the "base" for the run (line 23) might be problematic because this "boy" is not a single point on the line and instead covers a few squares beyond the line. Therefore, her explanation might not work well when the coordinate axes are introduced. Furthermore, the gradient of a line is calculated by considering the gradient of a line segment, and different line segments of the same line give the same gradient. While these notions may seem trivial, they are critical for students to understand the concept of gradient. However, she insisted that the difficulty identified was "trivial" and could be overcome with sufficient practice. Hence we see here some opportunities for a knowledgeable other to guide Anita to see from her students' perspective.

## Potential challenges in *kyouzai kenkyuu*

As highlighted in the preceding snapshots, countries outside of Japan that want to incorporate *kyouzai kenkyuu* in their lesson study practice often face several challenges. For some countries, the curriculum guides (which include textbooks, workbooks and other instructional materials from the Ministries of Education) are seen as sacrosanct, and teachers often follow them in prescriptive ways even though they are merely guidelines. Teachers should realize that they need to make changes to them according to the contexts of the schools and students they teach instead of seeing themselves as merely curriculum implementers who show unwillingness to deviate from these curriculum guides. Perhaps they are simply too busy to think about potential and different uses of these curriculum guides? Perhaps they do not have access to or little time to look for new resources and materials? Or perhaps the curriculum guides give them a sense of security, especially when they are unclear and uncertain about the subject matter of what they are teaching? Whatever the case may be, it is critical for teachers to think outside the box and interrogate the curriculum guides and materials available to them during *kyouzai kenkyuu*. Doing so will empower teachers to redesign instructional materials in ways that are more appropriate for their students by anticipating students' thinking and misconceptions. This can potentially bring about better student learning. The role of the knowledgeable other is important in supporting teachers during the *kyouzai kenkyuu* process. Schools would need to find partnerships with teacher education institutes, universities, professional organizations, teacher agencies and ministries of education, as these provide potential sources of knowledgeable others. It takes time for teachers to engage in *kyouzai kenkyuu*. One discussion is sorely inadequate, as the work of curriculum making may take several weeks. If teachers find that *kyouzai kenkyuu* is invaluable in helping them develop better in their subject matter knowledge and pedagogical content knowledge, they will be willing to invest time. However, schools are busy places, and we cannot add something to it without taking out something. It is important for schools to examine the work of teachers and reduce unnecessary administrative work and to give priority to the *kyouzai kenkyuu* phase of a lesson study cycle.

## Concluding remarks

The description about how teachers engage in *kyouzai kenkyuu* in the two cases in this chapter reveals how it works to develop teachers as collaborative professionals (Hargreaves & O' Connor, 2019), making curriculum and pedagogical decisions to influence student learning. The creation of "actionable artefacts" through the *kyouzai kenkyuu* phase of lesson study has made the collaborative thinking of teachers visible, shareable and improvable and could be used for ongoing iteration and future application. Engaging in *kyouzai kenkyuu* is not an easy task, and it is an uphill journey for schools outside of Japan as it is not embedded in the culture of schools. But *kyouzai kenkyuu* is necessary to bring about effective lesson study that will impact teachers' pedagogical content knowledge and improve student learning in classrooms. It is important for school leaders to provide time and space for teachers to engage in curriculum making through *kyouzai kenkyuu* to see the progression from the planned curriculum to its enactment and observe how students experience it in a spiral iterative process. Teachers would need to see the *kyouzai kenkyuu* phase as an inquiry process as they grapple with the why, what, who and how of teaching and learning during their collaborative discussions and examine the subject matter through the eyes of their students, anticipating their thinking and misconceptions. They would need to also examine available instructional materials and literature relevant to their research theme and redesign lessons and learning activities with supporting resources to meet the learning needs of their students. It is only through such collaborative discourse among teachers supported by "knowledgeable others" that reform ideas can take root in classrooms and bring about lasting change (Lee & Lo, 2013).

## Additional materials

Choy, B. H. (2015). *The FOCUS framework: Snapshots of mathematics teacher noticing* (Unpublished doctoral dissertation). University of Auckland, New Zealand.

Choy, B. H. (2016). Snapshots of mathematics teacher noticing during task design. *Mathematics Education Research Journal, 28*(3), 421–440. https://doi.org/10.1007/s13394-016-0173-3

Global Education Resources. *Tokyo Shoseki math textbooks (grades 1-9)*. Retrieved from www.globaledresources.com/media/products/books

Hargreaves, A., & O'Connor, M. (2019). *Collaborative professionalism: When teaching together means learning for all*. Thousand Oaks, CA: Corwin Press.

Jiang, H., Choy, B. H., & Lee, C. K.-E. (2019). Refining teaching expertise through analysing students' work: A case of elementary mathematics teacher professional learning during lesson study in Singapore. *Professional Development in Education*, 1–20. https://doi.org/10.1080/19415257.2019.1634624

Lee, K.E.C. (2019). Going deeper into lesson study through *kyouzai kenkyuu*: A case from Singapore. Paper presented at the *Annual Focal Meeting of the World Association of Education Research*, 5–8 August, Tokyo, Japan.

Lee, K.E.C., & Lo, M. L. (2013). The role of lesson study in facilitating curriculum reforms: Guest editorial. *International Journal of Lesson and Learning Studies, 2*(3), 200–205.

Lee, M. Y., & Choy, B. H. (2017). Mathematical teacher noticing: The key to learning from lesson study. In E. O. Schack, M. H. Fisher, & J. A. Wilhelm (Eds.), *Teacher noticing: Bridging and broadening perspectives, contexts, and frameworks* (pp. 121–140). Cham, Switzerland: Springer International.

Lim, C., Lee, K.E.C., Saito, E., & Syed Haron, S. (2011). Taking stock of lesson study as a platform for teacher development in Singapore. *Asia-Pacific Journal of Teacher Education, 39*(4), 353–365.

Melville, M. D. (2017). *Kyouzaikenkyuu: An in-depth look into Japanese educators' daily planning practices* (MA Unpublished thesis). Salt Lake City, UT: Brigham Young University. Retrieved from https://scholarsarchive.byu.edu/etd/6515

Ministry of Education, Singapore. (2014). *Science syllabus (primary)*. Singapore: Ministry of Education.

Shimizu, Y. (1999). Aspects of mathematics teacher education in Japan: Focusing on teachers' role. *Journal of Mathematics Teacher Education, 2*(1), 107–116.

Watanabe, T. (2002). Learning from Japanese lesson study. *Educational Leadership, 59*(6), 36–39.

Watanabe, T., Takahashi, A., & Yoshida, M. (2008). Kyouzaikenkyuu: A critical step for conducting effective lesson study and beyond. In F. Arbaugh & P. M. Taylor (Eds.), *Inquiry into mathematics teacher education* (pp. 131–142). San Diego: Association of Mathematics Teacher Educators.

Yang, Y., & Ricks, T. E. (2012). How crucial incidents analysis support Chinese lesson study. *International Journal for Lesson and Learning Studies, 1*(1), 41–48. https://doi.org/10.1108/20468251 211179696

Yokosuka, K. (1990). *Jugyokenkyu yougo daijiten.* (Dictionary of lesson study terms). Tokyo, Japan: Tokyo Shoseki.

Yoshida, M. (1999). *Lesson study: A case study of a Japanese approach to improving instruction through school-based teacher development* (Unpublished doctoral dissertation). Chicago, IL: University of Chicago.

Yoshida, M. (2011). *Conducting lesson study effectively*. Paper presented at the Tenth Annual Lesson Study Conference: Bringing the Common Core Standards to Life, Chicago, IL.

Yoshida, M., & Jackson, W. C. (2011). Ideas for developing mathematical pedagogical content knowledge through lesson study. In L. C. Hart, A. Alston, & A. Murata (Eds.), *Lesson study research and practice in mathematics education* (pp. 279–288). New York, NY: Springer.

# 6 Refining the research lesson's instructional approach during lesson study
## Mock-up lessons

*Shelley Friedkin*

> When teachers try to explain to each other their lesson plans, it is not really alive and so it is hard for the team to meaningfully discuss whether it is going to work or not. By having a mock-up lesson, we have the opportunity to experience what it feels like for students.
> —Fourth-grade teacher, Oakland, California

The mock-up lesson occurs when the lesson plan is finalized and the lesson study team has agreed on the lesson goals and task, anticipated student responses and planned out the flow of instruction. During the mock-up lesson, the research lesson instructor tries teaching the lesson or key elements of the lesson, with lesson study team members taking on the roles of different students. By taking on these perspectives, team members and the instructor can notice elements of the lesson they might have missed during the planning process. Lesson study teams find it useful to conduct a "mock-up lesson" just prior to the research lesson (see Figure 6.1).

In the San Francisco Bay area, the idea of a mock-up lesson was introduced in 2016 as a way to address the gap between the student learning goals described in the lesson plan and the learning that actually occurs during the research lesson. The relationship between writing a plan and teaching it (or "knowing" and "doing") is not simple: one does not easily equate to the other (Cochran-Smith & Lytle, 1999). Figuring out how to use what one knows for teaching is a complex process in which all teachers engage. It requires mathematical knowledge for teaching, the study of instruction and pedagogy, and time devoted to develop, test, and refine teaching (Ball, 2006). It also requires the ability to reflect on learning as learning

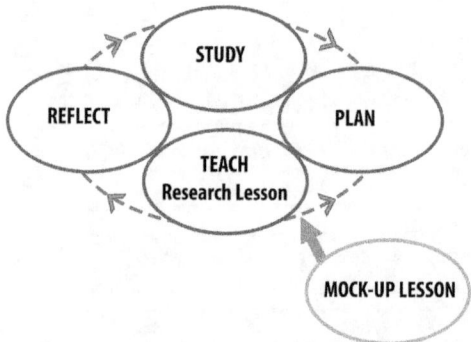

*Figure 6.1* The mock-up lesson as part of the lesson study process

is taking place (Schon, 1995). The mock-up lesson allows teachers to collaboratively engage in the complex process of making connections between knowing and doing. It provides a rehearsal opportunity where time is afforded to slow down the act of teaching for examination alongside student sense-making.

The mock-up lesson situates itself in a place where learning is brought to life for students. It provides teachers the opportunity to make sense of the relationships between the planned learning and how the learning plays out, based on the intended student outcomes. For example, as a rehearsal opportunity, the mock-up lesson allows the team to test out and refine their hypothesis about how teaching and learning can lead to specific student outcomes. This can only happen because the team has a well-developed understanding of the progression of expected student learning both across a unit and more specifically for the research lesson. The flow of instruction, the introduction of the task, anticipated student responses, areas of difficulty for students, learning goals and key points of evaluation have all been carefully considered. The team can pause the mock-up lesson to discuss teaching moves, ask questions, clarify, reflect, make connections and further rehearse, whereas during the actual research lesson this is not possible. As such, the mock-up lesson, when part of the lesson study process, brings together a pivotal learning experience that is closely aligned to the actual work of teaching.

---

**Thinking point**

How might your lesson study team use the mock-up lesson? Where in your planned flow of instruction do you want to test out and refine ideas about student learning and teaching?

---

In the remainder of this chapter, two cases are presented that illustrate the complex relationships between the planned learning for students, how it is enacted and what students learn. The cases show how mock-up lessons develop teacher sense-making and reveal high-leverage areas of focus that teachers choose to improve as they carefully consider student learning.

### Case one: progression of students' conceptual understanding of area

The first case focuses on a mock-up lesson designed to build the foundational concepts of area in order to support students' understanding of volume. The lesson study team explore the fifth-grade content standards taken from the Common Core State Standards–Mathematics, 5th grade, Introduction, Point 3:

> Students recognize volume as an attribute of three-dimensional space. They understand that volume can be measured by finding the total number of same-size units of volume required to fill the space without gaps or overlaps. They understand that a 1-unit by 1-unit by 1-unit cube is the standard unit for measuring volume.
> 
> (National Governors Association Center for Best Practices, 2010a).

The team also considers data from student assessments, where they learn that the fifth-grade students (selected for the research lesson) cannot accurately use an area formula (length × width) and the majority of students do not know how to calculate area accurately by any means. Having studied how students' understanding of volume relies on their understanding of area, and having explored many common misconceptions students have when approaching this topic, the team decides a vital interim outcome for students is to develop a conceptual understanding of area before moving on to volume.

Based on this information, the team selects a task from a series of activities called "Candy Boxes" by Marilyn Burns. In this series, students learn about models they can use for multiplication, explore rectangular arrays and build the concept of measuring while researching how to package candies. The candies are 1-inch-square tiles and are packed one layer deep in rectangular boxes. For the research lesson, the team adapts a task that provides students with a 7 in. × 5 in. box and three 1-inch-square tiles and prompts: "There are three candies in this box. The box was full. How many candies were there in the box to start?" The purposeful design of the instructional flow of the lesson involves the teacher presenting the problem; students then individually attempt to solve the problem using the materials provided and record their thinking in a math journal. After the students' independent think-time, the teacher facilitates a whole-class discussion where students share their thinking and the class collectively agrees on what they learned. This instructional flow was taken from a Teaching Through Problem-Solving approach to mathematics learning (McDougal & Takahashi, 2014) that students had established in their classroom.

## *Student's prior knowledge*

In preparation for the mock-up lesson, the students' classroom teacher shares with the team the student responses she anticipates. She also predicts which of her students will produce each type of response (see Figure 6.2).

---

Student response type A (7 students):
These students will have a hard time conceptually understanding the problem without having enough tiles to fill the box completely. They may need more tiles than the initial three given to solve the problem.

Student response type B (4 students):
These students will rely heavily on the tiles to figure out how many square inches are in the box. They may recognize that they can find out how many tiles are in one row, and then add the row totals together (repeated addition) to find the total number of tiles in the box

Student response type C (6 students):
These students will rely on the tiles to figure out how many square inches are in the box. They will use the tiles to measure the length and width, connecting their prior knowledge of rows and columns in arrays. They recognize they can multiply how many tiles fit in one row by one column to find the total number of tiles.

Student response type D (2 students):
These students will make the connection between using the tiles to measure how many square inches are in the box and using the ruler. They will measure the length and width of the box and connect this to their previous experience with arrays, multiplying rows by columns to find the total number of tiles and may refer to this as how many square inches the box measures.

---

*Figure 6.2* Anticipated student responses

*Refining the research lesson's approach* 55

With such a wide range of prior knowledge in the classroom, the team decides to use the mock-up lesson to explore how to leverage the students' anticipated responses to develop a conceptual understanding of area. They agree that students need to see how area is calculated, starting with a concrete representation where the space inside the box can be covered by iterating the unit to cover the entire space. After this, students connect this idea incrementally to more abstract representations of length × width.

### Seeing the mathematics

The board plan in Figure 6.3 is the final result of the team's work during the mock-up lesson. The mock-up lesson took one hour and ten minutes. First, the team thinks carefully about the new learning they expect all students to understand by the end of the lesson. This new learning for students is seen in the "Summary" on the board plan (see Figure 6.3): "We learned we can measure the area of an array using the length and the width". Reaching early agreement about the summary of the focal learning for all students allowed the team to consistently anchor their instructional decisions going forward.

> **Thinking point**
>
> How important is it for your lesson study team to reach agreement about the focal learning of the lesson for all students? Why might having this focal learning articulated be helpful during the mock-up lesson?

The representations in Figure 6.3 go through several iterations before being finalized. The changes the team makes are a result of the connections they discuss as they consider both anticipated student responses and how students might explain the strategies they use to solve the problem. An example of how the team changes their board plan as they think carefully about student type B's response is shown in Figure 6.4.

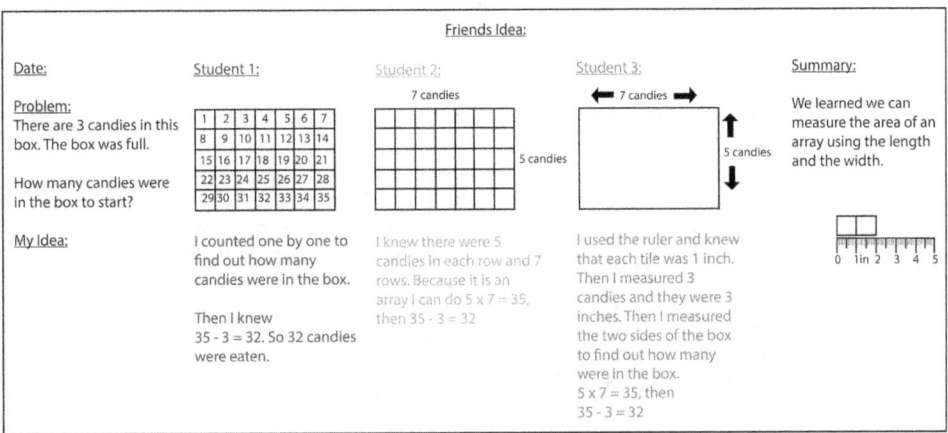

*Figure 6.3* Board plan after the mock-up lesson

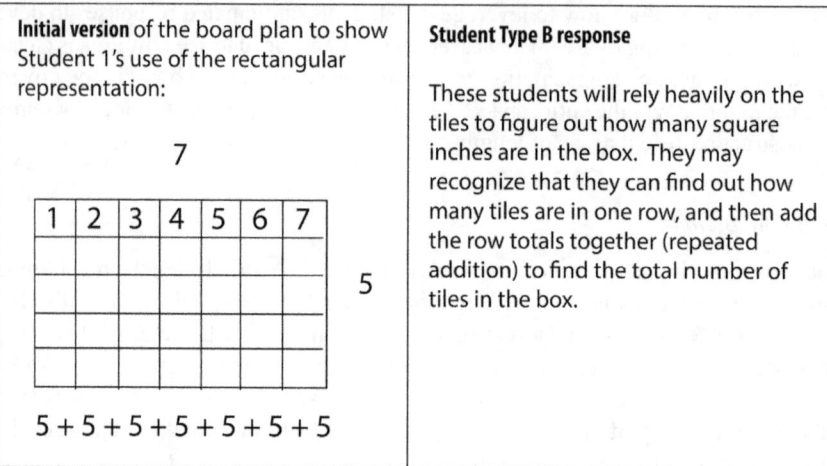

*Figure 6.4* Initial version of the board plan based on student type B's anticipated response

The team next mocks up student type B's mathematical expression for the area as 5 + 5 + 5 + 5 + 5 + 5 + 5 and discuss how to show this student's thinking using the rectangular representation. They also develop specific questions to probe students throughout the lesson ("back-pocket questions"), readily available for the instructor to use.[1] Such questions serve several purposes. First, they push the students to make explicit their thinking about the mathematics. Second, they make public specific understandings important for the whole class to hear. Lastly, they keep the agency of the mathematics with the student, as students (and not the teacher) answer the questions and therefore communicate the mathematical knowledge.

Through mocking up the student strategies on the board, the team can see how the big mathematical ideas they intend for students to grasp during the lesson come to life. They also become aware that the mathematical ideas needed to support student type A's response has not yet been addressed. As such, they revise the board work to show the use of the rectangular representation to help student type A understand that area requires the covering of the space with consistent size units (see Figure 6.5).

| Final version of the board plan to show Student 1's use of the rectangular representation: | Student Type A response |
|---|---|
| | These students will have a hard time accessing the conceptual understanding of the problem without having enough tiles to fill the box completely. These students may need more tiles than the initial three given to solve the problem. |

*Figure 6.5* Board plan for student type A responses

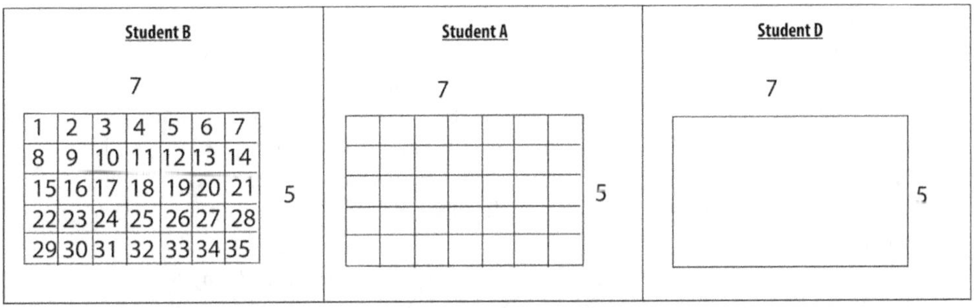

*Figure 6.6* Progression of three student responses

By rushing student type A into seeing the relationship between the rows and columns, the team concludes they are potentially robbing this student of the opportunity to connect their current thinking and approach to more sophisticated ideas about calculating area to come later in the lesson. The team changes the board plan for student type B's response to that shown in the final version of the board (see Figure 6.3). The team continues to think about student types A and D responses, drawing and labelling representations and surfacing more explicit back-pocket questions.

As the team looks across the three selected student responses on the board (see Figure 6.6), they see clearly the progression of the concept of area through the presentation of the rectangle and different ways of measuring its area. However, they still wrestle with how to handle the relationship of candies to tiles to 1-inch by 1-inch (1-inch-square) units. The three student representations on the board have "7" written on the top of the rectangle and "5" on the right side as shown in Figure 6.6.

Looking at student type D's representation, the teachers discuss:

*T1*: [As lesson teacher to student D] How did you know that each candy was 1-inch?
*T2*: [Taking on the perspective on student D] I used my ruler and I measured and saw that each tile was an inch.
*T1*: [As lesson teacher] Can you show me how you measured it?
*T1*: [To team members] Should the student be showing how they measured the tile with the ruler or the box?
*T3*: I don't think students will make sense of the length if the student just measures one 1-inch tile and shows it alongside the ruler.
*T2*: [Taking on the perspective of student D and stands up] I can show it like this [holding up the ruler and putting the tile up against the 1-inch mark on the ruler, and reiterating the inch along the edge of the ruler carefully increasing by 1 inch at a time]: 1 inch, 1 inch, 1 inch. I can also show alongside the candy box. [She starts reiterating the 1-inch tile alongside the candy box.]
*T4*: Can we show the connection of how we are describing the unit using the representations on the board?
*T2*: Oh yes, we are moving away from the grid for student D and . . .
*T4*: [Gets up and moves towards the board and points towards student D's rectangle without grids.] You can write in inches here [points next to the 7] and draw a line showing the 7 represents the length of this side [runs his finger along the top of the rectangle].
*T1*: [To team members] So this is 7 inches [draws in the line T4 suggested].

T3: As students are up at the board, some may say candies, some may say inches, some may say tiles?
T1: [To team members] So if they say inches, I'll say, "but I thought we are talking about candies", and get them to explain. If they say candies, I'll say, "but student D is saying they are inches", and I'll push them to explain. [Stands back and looks across the student responses] And here [points to student A's rectangle] I should write in "candies".
T2: And this can help the students see how candies or tiles are measured in inches.
T4: The first rectangle shows counting the tiles up to 35; students have not yet made explicit what the 7 and 5 are.
T1: [Erases the 7 and 5 next to student B's rectangle on the board] Okay.
T3: But they may say it though, they may see the quantities in each row and say 7 or 5.
T1: If they don't say it, it makes the progression really nice.

The adjustments to the visual representations play a critical role in supporting students to see the relationship between the candies in the question, the representation of the 1-inch-square tile, and the measurement of length and width with a ruler.

During this mock-up lesson, a coherent experience for students to support their sense-making around increasingly abstract mathematical ideas accompanied by precise notation is designed. Importantly, throughout the mock-up lesson the team repeatedly acknowledge that although they are planning out the enactment of the lesson in detail, they must allow the learning on the day of the research lesson to play out potentially in other ways, or for students to share responses the team had not anticipated.

### Thinking point

Why do you think it is important for the instructor of the research lesson to be prepared to abandon the carefully scripted board plan or selection of anticipated student responses on the day of the research lesson?

Case one highlights the affordances the mock-up lesson provides for the teacher of the research lesson and the lesson study team members to slow down instruction and think carefully about how they are operationalizing their learning goals. The focused time spent by the team examining teaching and learning is grounded in the board work and in visual representations that help students reason mathematically. By examining how students might make sense of the task, charting out student responses and then reasoning across student responses, the team becomes clearer about the high-leverage mathematical ideas and use of representations likely to support student learning. This clarity enables the development of appropriate probing questions to ask students to ensure the key mathematics of the lesson come from the student and not the teacher. This case also exemplifies how the teams' understanding of students' prior knowledge can support the appropriate use of student thinking during instruction to bring about the desired student learning outcomes for all students.

### Case two: developing a problem-solving lesson to understand equivalent fractions

The second case focuses on a mock-up lesson conducted by a team of district math coaches. The coaches create a lesson study team with a goal to better understand the process teachers experience when they use the district curriculum to support a Teaching Through Problem-Solving lesson (McDougal & Takahashi, 2014; Takahashi, Lewis, & Perry, 2013). This approach typically has four phases: posing the problem (brief); independent problem-solving (5–20 minutes); presentation, discussion and synthesis of students' ideas (15–30 minutes); and then the summary and reflection (brief). What is unique to a Teaching Through Problem-Solving (TTP) lesson is that students initially grapple independently with a novel problem and develop their own solution strategies before hearing others' ideas. During the next phase of the lesson, selected students present and explain their work to the class. The teacher carefully chooses and sequences these student presentations in order to highlight key ideas in the mathematics.

The team elects to focus their problem-solving unit and research lesson on equivalent fractions, a fourth-grade topic students often struggle to understand and teachers find difficult to teach well. The fourth-grade content standard they investigate is from the Common Core State Standards for Mathematics, 4.NF.1:

> Explain why a fraction $a/b$ is equivalent to a fraction $(n \times a)/(n \times b)$ by using visual fraction models, with attention to how the number and size of the parts differ even though the two fractions themselves are the same size. Use this principle to recognize and generate equivalent fractions.
> (National Governors Association Center for Best Practices, 2010b)

While the coaches do not have their own classrooms, in the research lesson classroom the student assessment data reveals that most students can name equivalent fractions for one-half when given a set of numbers (3, 4, 6, 8). In contrast, only four students out of twenty-two can name two equivalent fractions between 0 and 1. The team also reviews research to find out typical students' misconceptions surrounding equivalent fractions. An excerpt from their lesson plan reveals their learning (see Figure 6.7).

The team spends two hours and ten minutes on their mock-up lesson. As they start the mock-up lesson, they articulate the student outcomes they plan to meet by the end of the lesson: students will be able to connect a visual model (in this case an area model of equivalent fractions) to see the connection to multiplication (for example, why fraction $a/b$ is equivalent to a fraction $(n \times a)/(n \times b)$).

---

A huge percent of 4th and 6th grade students, when polled, were unable to recognize equivalence when asked to compare two equivalent fractions and many students thought that 10/12 was twice as large as 5/6, even though they knew how to find equivalence with the algorithm (McNamara & Shaughnessy, 2010). One potential reason for this is the overreliance on fraction manipulatives to teach equivalence. Manipulatives can eliminate the need for students to think about the mathematical relationship of equivalence (Empson & Levi, 2011). Additionally, the use of manipulatives, such as fraction bars, can be imprecise and lead to confusion about exact equivalence or estimated equivalence. Another misconception that happens due to a premature introduction of the algorithm for equivalence is the notion that a fraction is two separate numbers rather than a single number with a single value. For example, students will think of division by 3/3 as dividing by two separate whole-numbers as opposed to dividing by one (Empson & Levi, 2011).

---

*Figure 6.7* Excerpt from the team's research lesson plan, page 3

> **5. Stretch your Thinking.** Omar cuts a pizza into 4 slices and takes 3 of the slices. He says that he would have the same amount of pizza if he cut the pizza into 8 slices and takes 6 of the slices. Paul says he can cut the pizza into 16 slices and take 12 slices to have the same amount. Who is correct? Explain.
>
> *Math Expressions, 4th grade Unit 7, Lesson 4, Houghton Mifflin Harcourt Math Curriculum*

*Figure 6.8* Lesson problem

### Tasks that engage students in problem-solving

Elementary teachers in the district use a curriculum guide produced by the district's mathematics department. They also have access to *Math Expressions*, published by Houghton Mifflin. The task the team selects to adapt into a problem-solving lesson comes from *Math Expressions* (see Figure 6.8).

As the team of math coaches (MC) discuss the problem and the students they will teach, they share their plan to use an area model to help students understand that equivalent fractions have a greater number of smaller pieces or fewer larger pieces but take up the same area and have the same value. As an introductory activity to start their lesson, they plan to have students create three-fourths by folding the same sized piece of paper. Their rationale for this is the importance for students to use the same size wholes when proving equivalence. The team also wants students to think of pizzas as square-shaped and not just circular.

In attendance during this mock-up lesson is a visiting teacher, Mr. A. Mr. A has over twenty years of experience and is knowledgeable in using a TTP approach with students. After hearing the team's idea for the start of the lesson, Mr. A expresses some concerns:

*Mr. A*: In a problem-solving lesson, the problem you pose to students needs to activate their enthusiasm, questions and curiosity. You need to consider, is this task going to excite them? Have they done it before, and is it truly new mathematics for them? If you want students to fold paper and use a certain model, the situation should motivate students to do paper-folding or use a model rather than giving them step-by-step guidance; this does not let the students do the thinking.

*MC1*: I see. [Pause] So, what is a situation that requires students to break up pizza into smaller pieces and prove they are equivalent using a model?

*MC2*: Should we present the area models of pizza to them with a dilemma so they are working from the same model? We could simply ask them, do they want six pieces or do they want three pieces? [MC2 drew two area models as shown below.] And why?

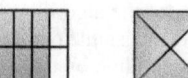

*MC3*: How do we then connect the pieces of pizza to fractions?
*MC2*: This is where language comes in. How are you naming the pieces?
*MC4*: And where the mathematics comes in. How can you prove it?

*Refining the research lesson's approach* 61

Mr. A: Yes, how will your students prove the shaded parts of the two shapes are equivalent?
MC1: Some could fold or cut them up and compare.
MC4: Would any look at the number of parts shaded and total parts?
Mr. A: This is the core mathematics that you want the students to discuss. Which shaded part is bigger, and how do you know?

The idea of using an area model to support students to see equivalent fractions continues to be central to the team's discussion. The research lesson teacher records on the board the student solutions selected by the team. They start with a student misconception to highlight the big mathematical idea that the size of the piece matters when comparing (see student 1's response below). As the mock lesson progresses, the team notes how important it is to provide student 1 the opportunity to review their original thinking along with any potential changes in thinking (as suggested by the star in the board plan in Figure 6.9).

Student 2's response reveals that area can be used to see if the six small pieces are the same as the three larger pieces. And, student 3's response focuses on the size of the pieces or the denominator. As in case one, team members carefully construct individual responses and also attend to the coherence and progression of the mathematics to be learned across the student solutions selected.

### *Core mathematics: proving equivalency*

The team reviews their board work and expresses satisfaction that the area model allows students to see equivalence between three-fourths and six-eighths, but they are still not convinced students will connect the area model of equivalent fractions to fractions as a value on the number line. Mr. A prompts a discussion:

Mr. A: At this point of the lesson, the students have used the area model and it seems like they are equivalent, but you want to push students. How do you know they are equivalent? In mathematics, we use a different approach to prove something is mathematically correct.
MC1: Ah, we could prove it using a number line.

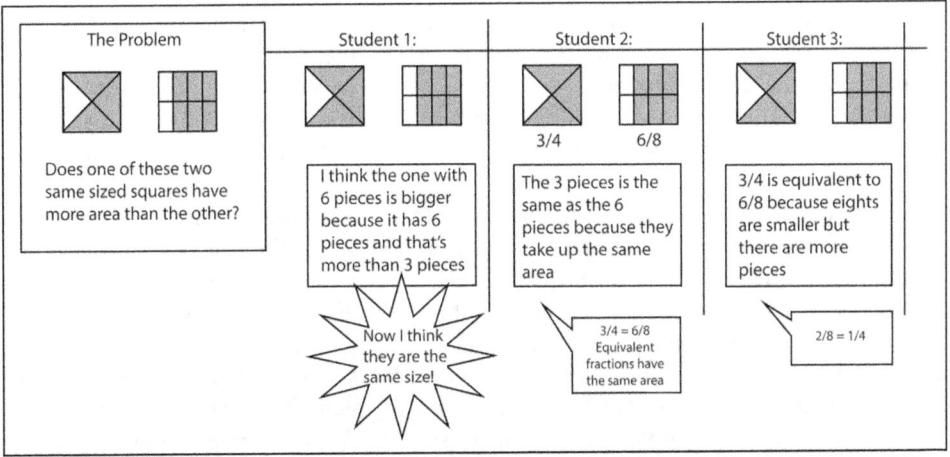

*Figure 6.9* Partial board plan during the mock-up

MC2: How would we show the different fractions on a number line?
MC4: We could use the fraction bars, lining them up.
Mr. A: Students can use this tool [the number line with fraction strips] to verify and they can discover if their projections are correct.
MC4: And they will all match up, allowing students will see they are at the same point on the number line.

The team realizes the key to support students' understanding of equivalent fractions is in proving that two fractions are equivalent. The area model is one way to visually see they take up the same area, whereas the number line proves the value is the same, as equivalent fractions occupy the same point on the number line.

There still remains concern by the team that students will not see the multiplicative relationship between the fractions. Returning to the mathematical standards (CCSS-M), the team notices the difference between student outcomes for Grade 3 and Grade 4. In Grade 3, students find two equivalent fractions, whereas in Grade 4 students find three or more equivalent fractions. Having just two equivalent fractions does not help students to see a pattern; in fact it is not possible to generalize a multiplicative relationship with just two equivalent fractions. Mr. A shares how he would encourage his problem-solving students to wonder if there are more than two equivalent fractions. He might pose the question, "What happens if we cut the pizza into smaller pieces; are there more equivalent fractions?" He suggests a third area model to capture students' problem-solving interest. Mr A draws the following on the board:

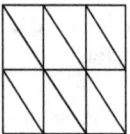

Team members are excited by the challenge this third model provides the students, and they decide to use it, posing the question: Can you shade [on area model 3] an equivalent fraction to three-fourths and six-eighths? The team notes that to do this, the students will need to first generate an equivalent fraction with smaller pieces by shading and then prove that it has the same area and that it occupies the same point on the number line as they did with the other two fractions. By the end of the mock-up lesson, the team is clearer about the flow of instruction, the incremental development of student learning and the types of outcomes that are likely to occur. They also have a deeper understanding of how the different representations can be used to push on students' thinking about equivalent fractions.

Several potential pathways for the instructor to move through the lesson are mapped out, with contingencies depending on the student thinking in the class on the day of the research lesson. If student 1's response does not appear, then they will start with student 2. If the students can prove equivalence for three-fourths and six-eighths using an area model, they will have students prove equivalence using a number line. If time permits, they will introduce nine-twelfths and encourage students to notice the pattern and eventually generalize the multiplicative relationship in equivalent fractions. The board plan in Figure 6.10 shows this complete story of the lesson and the development of the mathematics, along with expected student responses and the potential mathematical student learning outcomes.

*Refining the research lesson's approach* 63

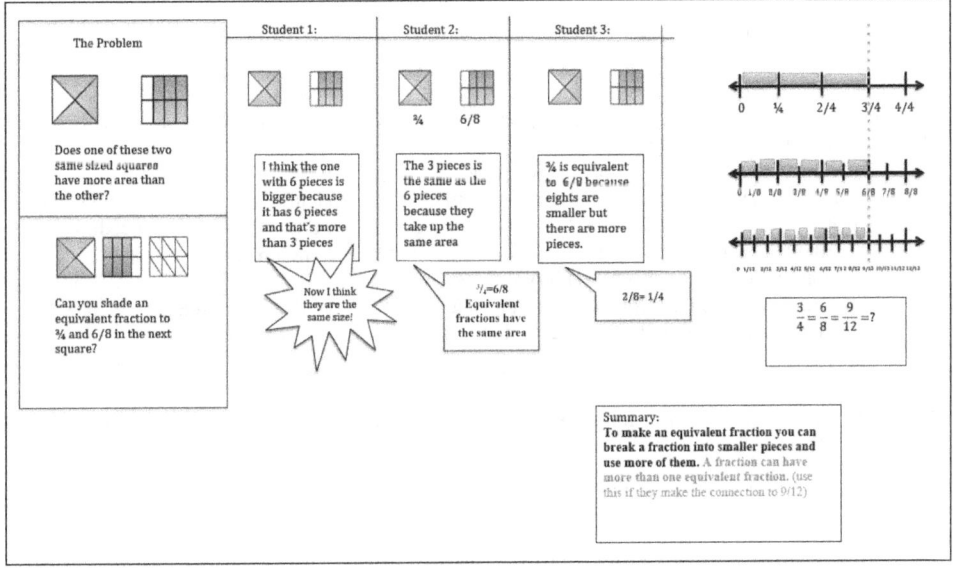

*Figure 6.10* Board plan after the mock-up lesson

**Thinking point**

Understanding the core mathematics and how student thinking progresses is key for this lesson study team. Do you think using the board to map out and discuss the core mathematical ideas and student responses is helpful? Why are visual representations important to student understanding in mathematics?

Looking back at the original word problem and reviewing the journey and adaptation it went through as a result of the mock-up lesson, it is easy to see how adding student thinking into the discussion adds complexity. Having a clear rationale for intended choices requires seeing the lesson from the students' perspectives. It also requires knowing how the core mathematics of the lesson can be built incrementally for student understanding and how different representations can be used to keep the construction of the mathematics with the students.

For this team, a deeper understanding of how the presentation of the problem, in a problem-solving lesson, needs to push students to the core mathematical ideas quickly in a keen and focused way was an "aha". Specifically, they reflected in their lesson plan: "We are no longer willing to teach a math lesson without thinking about the models and how they connect to the core mathematics. The model needs to match the math" (p. 14).

Interestingly, the findings from this lesson study cycle resulted in changes to the district's official curriculum, creating an important feedback loop where actual practice informed changes to the official curriculum. After the lesson study cycle was complete, the team of math coaches added a page to the district's published *Elementary School Guide to Examining Content and Unit Planning* (see Figure 6.11).

> Suggestions for Adapting a Math Expressions Lesson to Raise the Cognitive Demand and Make it More Student Centered:
>
> - Determine a mathematical goal for the lesson. Do not feel the need to teach the entire lesson as written! Less can be more.
> - Pick 1-2 problems to present during the lesson that address the mathematical goal.
> - Anticipate student responses for these problems. Allow students time to grapple with the problem on their own and develop their own strategies, rather than providing a procedure for them. Finally, select student work to share and compare, focusing on strategies that facilitate discussion that leads to the core math of the lesson.
> - At the end of the lesson, summarize the new learning. You can also give students a chance to revise their thinking or apply their new understanding to a new problem.

*Figure 6.11* Excerpt from district-published *Elementary School Guide to Examining Content and Unit Planning* document

## Conclusion

By including the mock-up lesson in the lesson study cycle, teams share how they experience a stronger connection to the teaching and learning proposed in the written lesson plan. They also value how the mock-up lesson allows team members to notice how the lesson feels from a student's point of view. After the mock-up lesson is complete and the instructor enters into the live research lesson, it is important to not allow the mock-lesson to become a script to follow during the live research lesson. It is at this point that the instructor must carefully listen to the student understanding as it presents itself during the lesson and craft the learning from this.

The mock-up lesson provides a pivotal opportunity, positioned right before the research lesson, to explore new ways of teaching and to refine instructional choices to promote student learning. Whether the team is focusing on the flow of the lesson, different types of student thinking, unearthing questions to promote student agency or reflecting on the design of the board to support the mathematical goal of the lesson, the extra time afforded to rehearse and discuss teaching is at the heart of what teachers do.

## Acknowledgement

With appreciation to the following teachers and mathematics coaches who shared their experiences and expertise, provided access to their written documents and gave permission for the videos of their mock-up lessons to be analyzed: Lisa Alley, Rashida Carter, Ruth Corley, Emily Flores, Sara Liebert, Robin Lovell, Ali Schneider, Justin Stoddard and Anita Summerlin. This work was funded through a grant from the Bill and Melinda Gates Foundation. The views, findings, conclusions and recommendations expressed herein are those of the author and do not necessarily express the viewpoint of the foundation.

## Note

1 Specific questions were "Where is the 5 coming from?" "Why are you adding the 5's together?" and "Why did you add this many 5's together?"

## Additional readings

Ball, D. (2006). Knowing and using mathematics in teaching. *Learning Network Conference: Quality, Quantity and Diversity*, 30–31 January, Washington, DC.

Cochran-Smith, M., & Lytle, S. L. (1999). Relationships of knowledge and practice: Teacher learning in communities. In A. Iran-Nejad & C. D. Pearson (Eds.), *Review of research in education*. Washington, DC: American Educational Research Association.

Empson, S. B., & Levl, L. (2011). *Extending children's mathematics: Fractions and decimals*. Portsmouth, NH: Heinemann.

McDougal, T., & Takahashi, A. (2014). *Teaching mathematics through problem solving*. Retrieved December 1, 2017, from www.nais.org/magazine/independent-teacher/fall-2014/teaching-mathematics-through-problem-solving/

McNamara, J., & Shaughnessy, M. M. (2010). *Beyond pizzas and pies: 10 essential strategies for supporting fraction sense*. Sausalito, CA: Math Solutions.

National Governors Association Center for Best Practices, & Council of Chief State School Officers. (2010a). *Common Core State Standards for mathematics (CCSS-M)*. Retrieved May 20, 2020, from www.corestandards.org/Math/Content/

National Governors Association Center for Best Practices, & Council of Chief State School Officers. (2010b). *Common Core State Standards for mathematics: Grade 5 introduction*. Retrieved May 20, 2020, from www.corestandards.org/Math/Content/5/introduction/

Schon, D. A. (1995). *The reflective practitioner: How professionals think in action*. Ashgate.

Takahashi, A. (2016). *Developing collaborative lesson research: Teacher professional development*, Summer Institute 2017, Bay Area, CA.

Takahashi, A., Lewis, C., & Perry, R. (2013). A US lesson study network to spread teaching through problem solving. *International Journal for Lesson and Learning Studies. International Journal for Lesson and Learning Studies, 2*(3), 237–255.

Takahashi, A., & McDougal, T. (2016). Collaborative lesson research: Maximizing the impact of lesson study. *ZDM Mathematics Education, 48*, 1–14.

# 7 Strengthening knowledge development in teachers' conversations in lesson study

*Edel Karin Kvam and Elaine Munthe*

## Introduction

Teachers who engage actively in lesson study cycles are committed to professional learning. They are also very aware of the responsibility they share with colleagues to ensure a best possible education of children and adolescents. This responsibility entails learning about and using updated and relevant subject matter knowledge and educational knowledge, and constantly seeking ways to improve and better understand teaching and learning. However, we know that the process of learning in groups can be challenging. These lesson study groups can function in ways that both enhance or impede possibilities for learning, or in ways that simply maintain a face value collaboration without digging deeper or challenging assumptions that bring on new learning (Horn & Little, 2010).

We understand professional learning as an act that entails active involvement with various kinds of knowledge. Through this active involvement, the production of shared knowledge for teaching and learning occurs. In line with sociocultural theory, we understand knowledge development as a social activity, mediated through language (Vygotsky, 1986). Language is not only understood as a tool for individual thought; language can also serve as support for a teacher community to construct common meanings together. In this way, conversations among teachers can help to change the boundaries of what they understand. Knowledge development is a dynamic process among teachers in their conversations.

In this chapter, we will discuss how teachers participate in developing knowledge processes as a basis for decision-making. All lesson study groups depend on language (or talk) as a medium for investigating, elaborating, challenging and learning. A main goal for this chapter is to contribute with theory and practical examples that can be useful when assessing the kinds of talk that go on in lesson study groups. This is essential for groups that wish to assess the ways they talk and develop their dialogic approach to knowledge development. We will first examine the role of knowledge in teaching and how conversations can contribute to bringing up diverse kinds of knowledge. We will then discuss how certain characteristics of teacher conversations can either increase opportunities for knowledge development or inhibit them.

## The role of knowledge in teaching

Teaching and learning are complex activities that take place within complex and diverse contexts demanding an equally diverse and complex knowledge base. On one hand, teaching relies on *practical knowledge*, which is expressed in actions and skills. In the research literature, various terms are used for practical knowledge, such as Ryle's "knowing how" (1949),

Eraut's "know how" (1994), Shulman's "strategic knowledge" (1986) and phenomena identified by Doyle as "classroom knowledge" (1979). Professional practice also relies on *scientific knowledge*, which means that teachers know that something exists. Such knowledge is also referred to as "propositional knowledge" (Shulman, 1986) and as "knowing that" (Ryle, 1949). A third area of knowledge is also of great relevance for teaching. Teachers will have to make decisions on various normative issues and continually make value decisions without clear rules and without anyone being able to make priorities for them. In some cases, there might be relevant evidence-based knowledge that can inform value decisions, but there can also be good reasons to apply different priorities or judgements. In many cases, teachers come across situations where conflicting values are at play. In such situations, there can be an urgent need for teachers to be able to exercise sound professional judgement.

Grimen (2008) uses the term *practical syntheses* to emphasize that it is through practical actions that different knowledge areas are combined and put into context in the actual work. In lesson study, teachers are involved in professional learning cycles that involve planning for learning. Munthe and Conway (2017) have described the activities and knowledge areas involved in planning as follows:

> When teachers plan lessons, they anticipate and design the framework and environment where learning will take place. They align goals, activities, and assessments in repeated cycles of planning, enactment, review, and re-planning. In line with Crick's definition of competence (2008), we can say that planning involves a complex combination of knowledge, skills, understanding, values, attitudes, and desire, and that these lead to effective action in the school.
>
> (p. 836)

What is at stake is the interaction between diverse knowledge areas and how they integrate in practical syntheses enacted in schools. Knowledge resources may originate from theory derived from different scientific disciplines, practical knowledge or familiarity with specific situations. It is the nature of the practical tasks that influences which knowledge elements are relevant to combine. It is the teachers themselves who must make this combination. We have experienced many situations where we are worried about a child's performance in school, both as teachers and teacher educators collaborating with teachers. The following is an example of such a dialogue. In this dialogue, we can see how the teachers are grappling with many issues related to motivation. They rely on their own practical experiences, but they also remember something they have read about motivation (scientific knowledge) and wonder how that can be helpful in their search for ways to help the child.

*Anne*: I still don't know what to do with Richard. You know . . . we've talked about this many times . . . but I haven't been able to get him going at all this year. He just sits there slouching.

*Paul*: What did his parents say? You talked to them?

*Anne*: Yes, I talked to them right after I talked to Richard . . . but they haven't really noticed any change and they say they have discussed his school work and he says everything is fine.

*Paul*: No . . . but . . . what does he like? It might be an idea to try to get him more motivated if he finds more pleasure or is more interested in what you're doing? Who was that – eh . . . the self-determination theory! Yeah – and the possibility for choice – that he is able to make some choices himself?

Based on a certain situation, a practical problem (Richard shows little motivation at school), the teachers create a synthesis of knowledge by combining different knowledge sources: a practical synthesis. These two teachers went on to discuss the kinds of learning activities that Richard was involved in, and they discussed how they could use collaborative learning principles in relation to the different situations they placed the pupils in, as well as their experiences with different kinds of collaborative practices. This need to combine different forms of knowledge is one of the distinguishing characteristics of teaching. Teachers need to master the interaction between various knowledge areas and be able to integrate them. Through practical syntheses where knowledge integration occurs, new understandings develop. When this is done collaboratively, for instance in lesson study groups, the possibility for shared professional knowledge development is evident.

## Exploring and challenging pedagogical practices by assessing the nature of the task

Lesson study is all about exploring and challenging pedagogical practices. Teachers investigate and test different ways of teaching the same topic and develop knowledge about their students' thinking, reasoning and understanding as well as their students' capacities. Teachers also develop insights into their own assumptions about students and students' capacities and learning and are able to challenge their own thinking and that of other colleagues.

To explore what to do and what knowledge is appropriate to use in a pedagogical situation, a starting point can be to explore the nature of the task. In the following excerpt from a conversation among sixth-grade teachers, a recurring problem was addressed (modified and translated from Norwegian by the authors; see Kvam, 2018a):

*Laila*: What we experienced before Christmas, what we were talking about, Martin. They [the pupils] don't score well on vocabulary. They don't take it seriously . . . learning the words. The best ones master the grammar, there's a sound development in English otherwise, but when it comes to vocabulary they don't put in much effort.
*Hilde*: They don't work on vocabulary?
*Laila*: No.
*Martin*: They don't practice enough.
*Laila*: We had a test every Friday throughout the autumn.
*Martin*: And even though they've been told, by their parents in fact, they choose not to practice [vocabulary].
*Liv*: It was the same last year, too. [Liv taught sixth-grade English the previous school year]
*Martin*: The only thing we can do is to ask them to practice. And if they don't practice, and they're well aware of it . . .

The recurring problem is that the students apparently did not learn the vocabulary that the teachers have decided they should. This was a problem that had been around for a while and seemed to occur every year. If the teachers decided to do a lesson study cycle on this topic, they could identify the task as "learning vocabulary" – but what was the nature of this task? What kinds of knowledge areas were relevant for the teachers to tap into when exploring and challenging existing practices?

In this case, the subject was English as a foreign language, since the students and teachers were based in Norway where English is taught from Grade 1, but the issue can also be related to all vocabulary learning. The teachers could start by assessing how they had gone about teaching vocabulary. What were the practices commonly used? What did we know about these practices? Could we assume that they were "effective" practices? If the problem kept occurring, might that be a clear indication that they were not effective? The teachers could turn to research to investigate whether there was any new knowledge about this topic. When doing so, they might come across a review conducted by Wright and Cervetti (2016). The authors of this review highlighted several problem areas related to not-so-effective practices and concluded that studies that actively teach students to monitor their understanding of vocabulary and the use of multiple, flexible strategies for solving word meanings are promising areas for future research. These were aspects that the teachers could investigate for future practice. However, the research review does not provide insight into all aspects. There might be students in class who do not have Norwegian as their first language. How would that matter for vocabulary learning in English? What about students with reading problems?

Discussions about the nature of the task provide opportunities for the teachers to explore each other's understandings and assumptions. Teachers can ask: what are the relevant assumptions to address or expose in this case; assumptions (i.e. personal theories or hypotheses) about how vocabulary is best taught; about how we learn vocabulary; about how particular students will engage in new activities or what are necessary opportunities for learning? Discussing assumptions and bringing them out into the open is an essential part of lesson study work. It requires that teachers are open and willing to share their assumptions.

Assumptions constitute a knowledge area that is important to explore and to challenge in relation to the task (or the goal) at hand. When starting to work in a lesson study group, it can be worthwhile to do this deliberately. Make it a point in the group's work. After some experience, it can become second nature. Based on our experience with lesson study groups, however, this can be a particularly challenging knowledge area to address. A reason to stress its importance is that when we make our assumptions explicit, we can also test them through the remaining stages of the lesson study cycle (observations and discussions based on what we experienced after trying something different). This can lead to more informed perceptions about what happens in teaching and thus stimulate collaborative and shared knowledge development.

---

**Thinking point 1**

Think about the last lesson study cycle you participated in:

How did you make your assumptions explicit?
Did you discuss your own personal theories?
Did you anticipate student thinking or behaviour?
How were you able to do that?

---

## Protocols for improving teachers' conversations

An important premise for knowledge creation through dialogue is that ideas, beliefs and feelings have to be explicit and available for exploration (Earl & Timperley, 2009). In other words, teachers must be courageous to let others comment on their incomplete ideas and have their own conclusions mirrored in the conclusions of others (Mercer & Dawes, 2008). This is about teachers giving each other space in the conversation, meeting each other as a "you" (Buber, 1992), in a climate characterized by trust and acceptance. Group members have to pay attention to which conversation characteristics open up and which ones close further exploration. Careful listening, asking questions, asking follow-up questions and including others' perspectives in the conversation are all relevant skills and features to develop and continually assess. Without these conversation characteristics, exploration may collapse and lead to something other than potential new insights.

Protocols for conversations (of which there are several), can be resources for the teachers. One example is the Cambridge Oracy Assessment Toolkit developed by Mercer, Warwick and Ahmed (2017). It was designed for improving student talk in schools, but it is also relevant for professionals at work. The toolkit includes assessment tasks and procedures for use by teachers together with a unique oracy framework for identifying the range of skills involved in using talk in any specific social situation. There are four strands of oracy described in the framework: physical, linguistic, cognitive, and social and emotional. The third area, cognitive, is made up of the following skills:

Cognitive

7  Content:

   a   a choice of content to convey meaning and intention,
   b   building on the views of others

8  Clarifying and summarizing:

   a   seeking information and clarification through questioning,
   b   summarizing

9  Self-regulation:

   a   maintaining focus on task,
   b   time management

10 Reasoning:

   a   giving reasons to support views,
   b   critically examining ideas and views expressed.

These are the skills that teachers teach their pupils to use, but they are also essential skills to be practised during teachers' exploratory talk and discussions during lesson study cycles regardless of which phase you are in.

The fourth dimension in the oracy framework is also relevant and can be developed by groups of teachers when deciding what their group norms of conversations should be:

Social and emotional

11 Working with others:

   a   guiding or managing the interactions,
   b   turn-taking

12 Listening and responding:

   a   listening actively and responding appropriately

13 Confidence in speaking:

    a    self-assurance,
    b    liveliness and flair

14 Audience awareness

    a    taking account of level of understanding of the audience.

A simple online search for "protocol + lesson study" will identify many protocols developed for use within lesson study groups. Many of the protocols are concerned with the phases of lesson study, but some are also more oriented towards the quality of talk that goes on within conversations.

---

**Thinking point 2**

Do you use a protocol for norms of conversations in your lesson study group?
How does the protocol help you explore your own thinking in your group?
Which other protocols may be interesting for you to try out and why?

---

## Engaging in critical conversations about pedagogical practice

However, merely making thoughts public and allowing them to stand side by side as equals is not sufficient for shared knowledge development. In lesson study discussions, this means that teachers should not only introduce multiple perspectives on the nature of the practical task, but they must also be willing to discuss their differing perspectives in a critical manner. They need to constantly assume that there is actually a better argument. This is what critical thinking entails, according to Dewey (1933). Teachers should maintain a state of doubt as they carry on systematic inquiry. When teachers engage in such critical discussions, they actively challenge each other's statements and do not simply engage in consensus-seeking behaviours. If teachers in their exploration do not look critically at the rationale behind the conclusions they drew together, the conversations may be limited to sanctifying "the good conversation", with the aim of the conversation being more of maintaining harmony than knowledge development (Løvlie, 1994, p. 21).

---

**Thinking point 3**

How can you take care of a good relationship with your colleague and at the same time give resistance to statements, arguments and perspectives?
What are some challenges you may face?

---

That conversations between teachers have a potential for knowledge development is documented in previous research. In a Norwegian context, Helstad and Lund (2012) have found that investigative negotiations in particular, where disagreements are expressed and challenged, can serve to promote knowledge development. These findings are also confirmed by international research in the field (see for instance Stoll, Bolam, McMahon, Wallace, & Thomas, 2006).

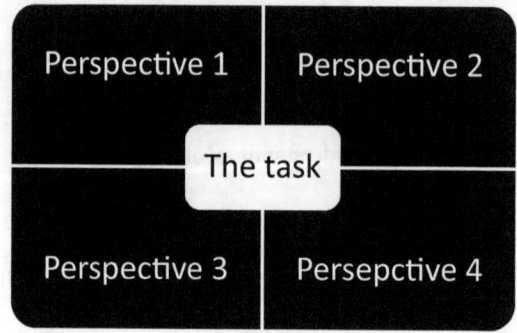

*Figure 7.1* Identify relevant perspectives needed to address the task at hand

However, research also shows that challenging each other in conversations can be difficult. Nemeth (2018) proposes the need to cherish dissent. Having a designated "devil's advocate" in a group is often suggested as a way to make sure there is some dissent in a group. But if this person does not represent true dissent, the critical issues brought up are easily overlooked. For a group to truly engage in critical discussions, a multitude of perspectives is needed.

In our case example, the group of teachers discussing students' engagement in learning vocabulary appeared to arrive at a consensus quickly. There was not much they could do but ask the students to study harder. This group probably landed in a rut where a pattern in their conversations had developed that allowed perspectives to be shared without deeper exploration. This did not have a driving effect on their knowledge development (Kvam, 2018a, 2018b). It can be challenging to ask critical questions about colleagues' conceptions of their practices, and perceived time pressures may emphasize the need for conclusions in schools rather than explorations. In some cases, it can be helpful for a group to draw a simple diagram such as the one in Figure 7.1 and to agree on some relevant perspectives that are needed to investigate a problem area or the nature of a task.

## Applying more knowledge resources in teachers' conversations

The introduction of new knowledge resources may play an important part in preventing teacher's practical work from becoming bogged down in habitual thinking, such as "fitting agreeably into a single picture or story" (Dewey, 1933, p. 13). Knowledge resources can be research, theory, lesson plans developed by the team or other teachers, education law, curriculum, and not least the groups' own systematic observations and knowledge about students' thinking and learning.

### *Knowledge resources from theory and research*

Scientific knowledge is not necessarily produced as knowledge that is ready for use by the practitioner. Theories are selected parameters – abstract systems – of phenomena. Since theories deal with phenomena as if they only consisted of the selected parameters, theories acquire general properties (Kvernbekk, 2005). We can also say that specific situations deal with more aspects than what particular theories can say something about. The relevance of theories for practical work is therefore something that teachers create themselves by relating theories to the specific context and situations. Theories must be processed and recontextualized to be relevant for use. (This also applies to knowledge resources which are not scientific.) In the case of "learning vocabulary", illustrated earlier, the nature of the task requires "knowing about", and the teachers need to investigate research and theory on vocabulary learning and what we know about this for the particular age group and the composition of students. Even empirical studies that examine the effectiveness of instructional methods can be difficult to implement directly without taking into consideration the new context. Teachers will need to translate the research to practice, find examples of how other teachers have addressed this task, and use other sources of knowledge about their students, about their context, about the resources they have available and so forth to plan approaches to teaching and learning. The effective translation of research relies on teachers being able to bring together "what is known" (i.e. formal knowledge) with what they know about their context, their students and what they currently see as effective practice (Brown, Malin, & Flood, 2019).

Theoretical knowledge is essential during all phases of lesson study, providing teachers with conceptual understanding of phenomena and a shared language that communicates beyond the particular group. Being able to discuss the nature of a task or a problem through a theoretical lens, for example being able to refer to self-determination theory or principles for collaborative learning, is a vital perspective for knowledge development and learning in a group. We can see the evident relevance this has for the planning phase, but it is also vital when determining how to observe, and which data to collect during the lesson, as well as when discussing observations and what was learned during this cycle that the group wants to share with others.

Discussing and determining which theories or which bodies of research knowledge could be important for the problem at hand can provide a foundation for the investigation topic in the lesson study cycle.

### *Knowledge resources from systematic data collection*

A challenging element in lesson study is to decide on a research question or decide on what in particular the group wants to learn something about. The topic under consideration needs to be "unpacked" as well and discussed from several perspectives (see Figure 7.1) so that it is clear what kinds of data will be needed to learn something on this topic. In most cases, teachers use observation as a tool, but what kind of observation is relevant? How have previous observations contributed to the groups' learning? Can they be developed further to enhance learning?

More experienced lesson study teams appear to use a broader range of data and have honed their observation skills through discussing actual observations and constantly referring back to the data they have on hand that can substantiate their claims. In this way, the teachers address questions of validity: how valid were the assumptions they put forward about students' thinking or their behaviour? By repeating lessons and refining lessons followed by systematic observations and other forms of data collection (student interviews, transcripts of student talk, etc.), teachers develop professional knowledge for teaching that involves the use of theories and research but has practice as the goal and the starting point. This is the "practical synthesis" mentioned initially, which is central for all professions.

Bocala (2015) studied lesson study groups that had little experience with lesson study and compared these with groups that had more experience. Her comparisons revealed some interesting differences (Table 7.1).

Table 7.1 Less developed and more developed forms of lesson study

|  | What teachers say they are learning | The purpose of classroom observation | The role of collaborative work |
| --- | --- | --- | --- |
| Less developed lesson study | Learning how to teach with problem solving | Watching other teachers to learn activities or ways to teach content | Planning with other teachers to produce one lesson |
| More developed lesson study | Learning the connection between teaching through problem solving and investigating student thinking | Observing to see the effect of pedagogy on eliciting student thinking | Generating collective understanding about students for revision, reflection and continuous learning about instruction |

Source: Bocala (2015, p. 358).

This study is, unfortunately, not a longitudinal one. The groups were different groups of teachers. We cannot say that the way they talked has changed. But what we might assume is that the ways the groups talked, the focus or nature of the task they investigated, the questions they asked and their own definition of what they wanted to learn were most likely quite different.

The process of moving from a less developed lesson study group to a more developed one is complex. It requires that group members "buy in" and are committed to learning and developing knowledge for their own good and for the good of others. A lack of critical dialogue between teachers can lead to conversations remaining at a superficial level, but there are several ways groups can join forces to ensure that lesson study contributes to professional learning and continuing school improvement.

> **Thinking point 4**
>
> Which knowledge sources do you use?
> How do you collect the data you need, and are these adequate?
> Is the quality of your data adequate for the kinds of discussions you need?
> Are there knowledge sources you tend not to use but which could be helpful?
> Do you spend enough time in the planning process, with opportunities to engage in critical conversations?

## Conclusion

In this chapter, we have discussed how teacher conversations can strengthen knowledge development. We have pointed to a number of challenges in teacher conversations that are not sufficiently explorative and which normalize existing teaching practices rather than challenge them. These conversations do not go in depth and are largely local knowledge processes without links to external knowledge resources. On the other hand, we have pointed out opportunities for conversations that could establish a more solid foundation for decision-making and even strengthening knowledge development. The biggest potential for knowledge development is probably when teachers in their exploration put both internal and external knowledge resources into play and identify and develop a pedagogical rationale for practice. Good teaching involves the assessment of what kinds of knowledge are appropriate to combine and which are critical to the development of effective tasks that will improve student learning.

## Additional readings

Bocala, C. (2015). From experience to expertise: The development of teachers' learning in lesson study. *Journal of Teacher Education, 66*(4), 349–362. https://doi.org/10.1177/0022487115592032

Brown, C., Malin, J., & Flood, J. (2019). Exploring the five key roles school leaders need to adopt if research-informed teaching practice is to become a reality. *Translational Research Insights, 2*(1–4).

Buber, M. (1992). *Jeg og du*. Oslo: Cappelens Forlag.

Dewey, J. (1933). *How we think: A restatement of the relation of reflective thinking to the educative process*. Boston: D. C. Heath.

Doyle, W. (1979). Making managerial decisions in classrooms. In D. L. Duke (Ed.), *Classroom management: The seventy-eighth yearbook of the National Society for the Study of Education* (pp. 42–74). Chicago, IL: University of Chicago Press.

Earl, L. M., & Timperley, H. (2009). Understanding how evidence and learning conversation work. In L. M. Earl & H. Timperley (Eds.), *Professional learning conversations: Challenges in using evidence for improvement* (pp. 1–12). Dordrecht: Springer.

Eraut, M. (1994). *Developing professional knowledge and competence*. London: Falmer Press.

Grimen, H. (2008). Profesjon og kunnskap. In A. Molander & L. I. Terum (Eds.), *Profesjonsstudier* (pp. 71–86). Oslo: Universitetsforlaget.

Helstad, K. & Lund, A. (2012). Teachers' talk on students' writing: Negotiating students' texts in interdisciplinary teacher teams. *Teaching and Teacher Education, 28*(4), 599–608.

Horn, L. S., & Little, J. W. (2010). Attending to problems of practice: Routines and resources for professional learning in teachers' workplace interactions. *American Educational Research Journal, 47*(1), 181–217.

Kvam, E. K. (2018a). *Laereres kollegasamtaler. Om profesjonalitet, laerersamarbeid og utvikling av bedre undervisning*. Oslo: Universitetsforlaget.

Kvam, E. K. (2018b). Untapped learning potential? A study of teachers' conversations with colleagues in primary schools in Norway. *Cambridge Journal of Education, 48*(6), 697–714.

Kvernbekk, T. (2005). *Pedagogisk teoridannelse. Insidere, teoriformer og praksis*. Bergen: Fagbokforlaget.

Løvlie, L. (1994). *Det pedagogiske argument*. Oslo: Cappelens Forlag.

Mercer, N., & Dawes, L. (2008). The value of exploratory talk. In N. Mercer & S. Hodgkinson (Eds.), *Exploring talk in schools* (pp. 55–71). Washington, DC: Sage.

Mercer, N., Warwick, D., & Ahmed, A. (2017). An oracy assessment toolkit: Linking research and development in the assessment of students' spoken language skills at age 11–12. *Learning and Instruction*. https://doi.org/10.1016/j.learninstruc.2016.10.005

Munthe, E., & Conway, P. (2017). Evolution of research on teachers' planning: Implications for teacher education. In J. Clandinen & J. Husu (Eds.), *The SAGE handbook of research on teacher education* (pp. 836–852). Thousand Oaks, CA: Sage

Nemeth, C. (2018). *In defense of troublemakers: The power of dissent in life and business*. New York, NY: Basic Books.

Ryle, G. (1949). *The concept of mind*. London: Hutchinson.

Shulman, L. S. (1986). Those who understand: Knowledge growth in teaching. *Educational Researcher, 15*(2), 4–14.

Stoll, L., Bolam, R., McMahon, A., Wallace, M., & Thomas, S. (2006). Professional learning communities: A review of the literature. *Journal of Educational Change, 7*(4), 221–258.

Vygotsky, L. S. (1986). *Thought and language*. Cambridge, MA: MIT Press.

Wright, T. S., & Cervetti, G. (2016). A systematic review of the research on vocabulary instruction that impacts text comprehension. *Reading Research Quarterly, 52*(2), 203–226. https://doi.org/10.1002/rrq.163

# 8 Scaffolding student teachers' professional noticing when using lesson study

*Gro Naesheim-Bjørkvik, Nina Helgevold, and Deborah Sorton Larssen*

## Introduction

Classrooms provide complex working environments which pre-service teachers may find overwhelming. At the University of Stavanger, Norway (UiS), lesson study (LS) was introduced as an integral element in the courses for pre-service teachers in English as a foreign language (EFL) and physical education (PE) to assist them in developing a more nuanced understanding of this complexity. Our experience and research have shown that LS supports pre-service teachers' professional development by making them more aware of the relationship between their teaching and pupils' learning. Some of our pre-service teachers have found it to be particularly challenging to develop good research questions or aims for their lesson studies. Often these aims were too general and difficult to study. In addition, the observations and reflections made during the research lessons tended to be superficial, thereby limiting the learning potential of engaging in LS. As teacher educators, we have been trying to strengthen the learning potential of the LS cycle by offering additional support to our pre-service teachers. We have grappled with the following questions: How can we support them in developing research goals that would drive the planning of their research lessons? How can we facilitate a deeper focus on the evidence of pupil learning during their observations of research lessons? How can we help them to connect these to principles of teaching and learning?

The concept of *noticing* (Mason, 2002, 2011) has guided our work. Noticing has been described as a component of expert practice, where teachers are sensitive to particular aspects of their work as well as techniques for analyzing, using and inquiring into these features of their practices. This involves observing classroom practices closely, analyzing crucial incidents and situations, and using evidence based on observations to guide future decisions about teaching. Van Es (2011) describes a developmental trajectory of noticing, including four levels: *baseline, mixed, focused* and *extended*. At level one (baseline), teachers are described as attending to the whole-class environment. At level two (mixed), they primarily attend to the whole-class environment, but they also begin to attend to particular students' thinking. Level three (focused) involves attending to particular students' thinking, and at level four (extended), teachers are able to attend to the relationship between particular student thinking and teaching. At level four, teachers are able to make connections between the events and principles of teaching and learning and on the basis of these interpretations propose alternative pedagogical solutions. Even though this framework is based on teaching mathematics, we think the descriptions of the different levels of noticing are useful in relation to the learning trajectory we want for our pre-service teachers when doing lesson study in PE and EFL. If we aim for our pre-service teachers to develop in the direction of level four, what kind of scaffolding do they need during the different stages in lesson study? How can we best support them in following this trajectory?

At our university, practicum and also LS are organized to allow small groups of pre-service teachers to share their teaching and observe each other in the classroom. This is facilitated by a school mentor who is required to observe their lessons and hold regular supervision meetings. During these meetings, the student group discusses their impressions of what they have observed, what they have discovered about pupils' learning in relation to the learning aim and activities chosen, and how this knowledge can be adapted and applied to future lessons. The difference between normal observations undertaken during practicum and LS observations is that the former tends to be on the whole class and/or the teaching. In relation to the noticing framework, such observations are often at level one or two and often lead to there being a focus on those pupils who are particularly noticeable in the class (those with special educational needs or whose behaviour is particularly obvious). During LS, case pupils are carefully selected and it is they who are observed, thus narrowing the focus onto those pupils that are necessary to observe in order to answer the research questions. We use case pupils during LS lessons to move the observations and later discussions during the supervision sessions beyond level two towards level three. During LS, three of the supervision sessions are set aside and take place at specified times during the cycle: before the research lesson, between the first and repeated research lesson and after the repeated lesson.

In this chapter, we present two cases, one from physical education (PE) and one from English as a foreign language (EFL), to illustrate the various tools we introduced aimed at providing scaffolding to develop undergraduate pre-service teachers' noticing skills when they are engaged in LS. Both these cases were from the autumn semester, when the third-year students undertook a three-week practicum during their five-year MA in education programme. The first case, from PE, introduces the use of a *kyouzai kenkyuu record sheet* (Seleznyov, 2016) during LS. The second case, from EFL, illustrates how *prompts* can be used throughout the LS cycle to encourage the students to dig deeper into the LS cycle as they progress through the process. Reflections on the use of these tools and future practices to strengthen the use of LS conclude the chapter.

## Introducing *kyouzai kenkyuu* record sheet – a case from physical education (PE)

In order to scaffold PE pre-service teachers in their development of professional noticing skills during the lesson cycle, we introduced the *kyouzai kenkyuu* record sheet. The idea behind the record sheet was to guide both the planning of the research lesson and the observations during the enactment of the research lesson. We also assumed that working carefully with the record sheet in the planning phase would drive deeper reflections and analysis of the research lesson during the post-lesson discussion phase of the LS cycle.

*Kyouzai kenkyuu* is a Japanese term which defines the "study of materials related to the research theme" or "the study of materials for teaching". Japanese teachers normally spend several weeks reviewing academic literature, curricula, textbooks, videos and other support materials in order to gain valuable information related to their research theme before they proceed with their lesson study. During this study phase, they discover elements of how pupils *normally* learn a topic and how this can be seen in light of their own pupils, curriculum expertise and resources. This is a necessary first step in lesson planning as it extends their knowledge of the topic and offers alternative activities that might be useful to consider. Our introduction of the *kyouzai kenkyuu* record sheet challenged mentors and pre-service teachers to discuss in what ways new material and knowledge about teaching and learning could connect, deepen and question their current knowledge and practices. It supported them in developing research questions and the kinds of focused observations needed for the research lesson(s).

*Before practicum*

Before the start of practicum, each student group contacted their school mentors to find out what potential learning aims could be considered during their practicum. They would gather more information about the challenges that their pupils may face with different learning aims and how they may respond to certain pedagogical approaches. Information about the contexts of learning, available equipment and resources and class culture (e.g. rules and rituals in the classroom) were important to find out. Using the record sheet as a guide, the students would begin to discuss with their mentor teacher(s) what possible research questions and types of lessons would yield useful data for their LS project.

Upon their return to campus and with the support of their university teacher, the pre-service teachers would then decide on their research question and begin to search for relevant curriculum materials and educational research so that they could deepen their content knowledge about this topic. Once the search was completed, the student groups would work together to discuss and agree on which of this material they want to use in their LS.

Table 8.1 shows an example of how one student group worked with the *kyouzai kenkyuu* record sheet. This group was doing their practicum as part of an exchange programme with a university in Valencia, Spain, and wanted to discover how to develop pupils' motor skills, (such as eye-foot, eye-hand and balance) whilst managing possible language barriers. Their research question was, "How to facilitate learning activities so that pupils develop coordinating motor skills (eye-foot, eye-hand, balance) when verbal communication is challenging?" Whilst studying the academic literature, the pre-service teachers became aware of the communicative possibilities within non-verbal and paraverbal communication. This led to exciting idea exchanges in the group about how they could find good exercises with eye-hand/eye-foot coordination that made such communication possible. With the help of their university teacher, they found two articles that revealed the communicative possibilities within non-verbal and paraverbal communication. They also found good examples of exercises to develop body balance and coordinating motor skills in textbooks as well as relevant videos on YouTube. The group discussed how the concepts discovered in these materials could improve communication in their teaching and how they could become more aware of the different forms of communication which could take place during teacher-pupil interaction.

The new information they gathered was applied to the development of the learning aims. In the discussion, they focused on the kinds of prior knowledge the pupils might have to help them reach the lesson aims and what the pupils might find difficult in the learning of the concepts to be taught. This required the LS group to re-examine their materials to check if there were any suggestions that might help them to predict how the pupils might respond. They further discussed how different forms of non-verbal and paraverbal communication might be applied using different exercises and music. As a result of these discussions, they decided to focus their observations on how these different forms of communications might affect pupil motivation and engagement during the lesson. The use of the *kyouzai kenkyuu* record sheet, together with the study of literature and other relevant materials, supported the pre-service teachers as they explored and defined the research lesson that would guide their LS research.

The following are some examples of research questions that other groups developed whilst using the record sheet. One group wanted to discover how soccer (football) could be used as

*Table 8.1* An example of a completed *kyouzai kenkyuu* record sheet

**What is the research question?**

How to facilitate learning activities so that pupils develop coordinating motor skills (eye-foot, eye-hand, balance) when verbal communication is challenging?

**What literature and support material did we find most relevant to our research question?**

Article 1: "Teachers Communication in a Physical Education Class" (Paxnhi, G. 2014)

Article 2: "How a theory of motivation can be used to develop a good learning environment in PE" (Jakobsen, A. 2012)

Textbook: Kvikstad, 2016. *Motor skills from a pedagogical perspective.*

Videos from YouTube.

**How do these materials about teaching and learning:**

| Connect with our own knowledge and practice? | Deepen our knowledge and practice? | Challenge our own knowledge and practice? |
|---|---|---|
| *Art 1*: How the use of communication when teaching a class will influence children's learning? In the article, Paxnhi elaborates on different ways of communication in use when teaching: verbal, paraverbal and non-verbal. According to Paxnhi, verbal communication only constitutes 7% of what is communicated, while the paraverbal constitutes 38% (e.g. your tone of voice, volume, speed). Finally, the non-verbal influences pupils' perceptions. *Art. 2*: Autonomy, competence and sense of belonging crucial for pupils' motivation. 3. Textbooks and videos which challenge our previous experience | *Art. 1*: To be more aware of how we as students communicate in different situations in order to improve teaching and learning. *Art. 2*: Illustrates inductive teaching in a very good way. The pupils will decide for themselves how to move through the trail. We as teachers will be mentors and instructors when this is needed. Support the pupils' balance between skills and challenges in a positive way. 3. Gave a lot of practical examples and good ideas. | *Art.1*: Since we will be teaching in a Spanish classroom, verbal communication will be challenging. We will try to be very aware of and plan how to use non-verbal communication in an explicit way. Body movements need to be clear in order to show/model activities. *Art. 2*: It will be challenging to make pupils aware of and be familiar with aims of the lesson. Constructive criticism and praise are essential for pupils' intrinsic motivation. When verbal communication is difficult, we have to plan other ways of communicating. 3. To prepare a suitable trail. |

Source: Adapted from Seleznyov (2016).

an appropriate learning activity in PE. Their research question was, "How can football be used in a way that includes everyone in the class and levels out ability differences?" They found several ideas from sources such as the local curriculum and the internet, for example, "ball game teaching in a theoretical education perspective". In addition, they used football textbooks (for teachers) and videos from YouTube, and they returned to practical learning activities they had experienced at university. The second group wanted to focus their research on how they could use more deliberate play in PE lessons to engage and motivate pupils who didn't like the subject. Their research question was, "How do deliberate play activities effect the level of motivation and engagement in a lesson?" In this example, the materials they used were the national and local curriculum, a research article and a textbook focusing on the importance of deliberate play in PE. They similarly used their own campus experiences where practical activities of deliberate play had been demonstrated and evaluated. Based on their work in the planning phase, they were able to design a research question, predict pupils' behaviour and plan observations of the research lesson accordingly.

## During practicum

Although the *kyouzai kenkyuu* record sheet together with the materials research was an invaluable aid in the planning and execution of the research lesson, its significance should not be underestimated in the post-lesson discussions which the pre-service teachers had with their mentor teacher. Deciding when and how to observe the different events during the research lesson and being more aware of how these had affected pupil learning offered opportunities to elaborate on these observations and make connections between events and principles of teaching and learning. These interpretations sometimes led to proposing alternative pedagogical solutions than the ones chosen. With the support of the work with the record sheet, the pre-service teachers (together with their mentor) seemed to have better noticed specific events which had occurred during the lesson rather than have a more general overview. As some of the student groups were undertaking an overseas practice, there were opportunities to compare the relevance of their research findings explored in a Spanish context to the Norwegian context. Based on their data interpretation, these pre-service teachers were able to make connections between the classroom events they had noticed and the principles of teaching and learning in PE in different contexts.

## After practicum

The pre-service teachers wrote up their LS reports, which included descriptions and reflections about the record sheets and the LS cycles and a detailed planning sheet for the lesson. Related to the record sheet shared earlier, one of the pre-service teachers commented:

> The curricula materials we discussed supported us in our planning of the lesson and really made us aware of communication as verbal, paraverbal and non-verbal. It also made us aware of the effect of chosen communication in certain situations and how to attend to different pupils.

Such pre-service teacher reflections can also be seen in the other groups. In one group, the record sheet seemed to establish a "common ground" for their research and collaboration during the LS cycle as they noted:

> The record sheet was a good basis for discussing and working with the research question in our group. It enabled us to think in a more structured way about what new knowledge the literature and the support materials for teaching could offer us and the teaching strategies. We suddenly understood how important it was to develop a good research question.

The other group noted:

> Through the record sheet, we have used relevant support material that helped us to look more critically at the research question and our teaching methods. We have expanded our experience-based knowledge. After these LS sessions, we feel that we succeeded in presenting [football] in a way that included and engaged all pupils, including those with less experience or special needs.

The *kyouzai kenkyuu* record sheet has scaffolded our pre-service teachers in a developmental trajectory of "noticing". In the next section, we will introduce the use of prompts in EFL as another tool to scaffold this trajectory.

## The use of prompts during the LS cycle in EFL

Pre-service teachers had undertaken an individual observation research assignment during the fourth semester's practicum and thus had some basic experience and understanding of doing classroom-based research before starting LS. However, doing an LS in the fifth semester was very different and more challenging. It entailed working together in a group and coming to joint agreement at all stages of the cycle. It also required a much deeper description and hence understanding of the theoretical rationale behind the research lesson activities so that they could begin to develop their understanding of the connections between teaching and pupil learning.

### *Before practicum*

At the start of their LS cycles, our pre-service teachers in EFL, like those in PE, needed to gather a considerable amount of information before they began their investigations and lesson planning. In cooperation with their school mentor, they needed to know about:

- The context of the classroom within the school (the grade they would be researching in, which classes will be involved and when the research lessons might be timetabled);
- The learners in the class (how many, where they were in their English abilities, what the range of these abilities were and their motivation for learning English);
- The learning aims as well as the content that were planned during their stay at the school.

This information gathering could only be done in cooperation with their school mentor who would know their classes and syllabus and could help the pre-service teachers by facilitating the timetable. Prompts at this stage were concrete and acted as reminders of questions they needed to discuss with their school-based mentors. For example:

---

- How many learners are there in each class, and what is the range of their English abilities?
- What is/are the learning aim(s) for this practicum, and what course books and additional materials are available for use?
- How many lessons of English will we have during practice?
- How long is each lesson and how are they timetabled?
- When will be the most appropriate time to schedule the research lessons?

---

Once the context of the lesson was known, the pre-service teachers could then make decisions about the learning aim they wish to focus on during their LS. The next set of prompts in this pre-planning phase asked them to explore and discuss the pre-knowledge that pupils may have and the possible challenges that the content of the lesson may give to all or any special needs children in the class. Although the pre-service teachers could use their background knowledge of classes they have taught in the past, the knowledge of their mentors was particularly invaluable. Such knowledge helped them predict how the pupils would respond to each lesson. The prompts suggested below helped pre-service teachers unpack their contextual knowledge, their general pedagogical knowledge and their subject specific knowledge in relation to the learning aim or content:

- What are the learning aims for this lesson, and why are these important?
- What prior knowledge of these aims and content do the pupils have that may help them?
- What potential difficulties may the pupils experience during this lesson?
- Does anyone in the LS group have experience of teaching these lesson aims/content before?

The discussion from these prompts allowed the pre-service teachers to identify a suitable challenge they would like to meet as a basis of their LS. This is a critical stage in the planning phase as it directed their review of curriculum and academic literature. Additional prompts helped them to clarify their research question and narrow down the possibilities for research to something which was appropriate within the time constraint of one lesson.

- From what you now know about the context and the challenges these learning aims may pose for some or all the learners, what may be interesting to research?
- What possible research questions may be possible to pursue in this single lesson?

Having agreed upon a possible research question, pre-service teachers could begin to investigate possible approaches to the teaching of the learning aim by reviewing curriculum documents, course books and supplementary materials. This would give them multiple ideas to choose from in planning their research lesson. It is important for pre-service teachers to collectively imagine what the lesson may look like and to tentatively predict how the pupils' learning and understanding of the aim could develop. Such discussions during the lesson planning phase would support pre-service teachers' ability to observe important events as they occur during the lesson. Prompts serve as scaffolds during this phase and would include questions which not only helped with the lesson planning but also in deciding what data to collect for subsequent lesson analysis as shown below.

There are prompts which can help not only in the planning the research lesson but also develop an inquiry stance towards a lesson:

- How can the learning aim be broken down and differentiated so that all the pupils are given the opportunity to learn?
- What is your rationale (theoretical basis) behind the choice of the activities and the way you have organized them?
- What must the focus of the observation and interview questions be so that the data collected will help to answer the research question?
- Do you need comparative data in order to test your research question (questionnaires, samples of writing, sound files, etc.)?

## During practicum

The three supervision sessions undertaken during practicum had very different foci. The first meeting had two main aims: the first was to focus on the lesson plan and the practicalities of executing and observing it in the classroom, and the second was to choose three or four research pupils who could be closely observed and possibly interviewed. It was important to predict how these research pupils would react to the lesson and imagine how their learning could develop.

In relation to the noticing framework, the aim of this supervision meeting was to facilitate opportunities for the pre-service teachers to focus their observations on case pupils rather than the class as a whole and nudge them towards level three. The intention was to lift the groups from a focus on the nuts and bolts of the lesson and how it could be taught towards a more reflective discussion of how the activities designed could lead to better pupil learning. The next set of prompts helped the pre-service teachers to be aware of the times during the lesson when the case pupils would show interesting and important learning behaviours.

- Which pupils should you focus on for your observations in order to collect data in response to your research question (e.g. ability levels or special challenges)?
- How will the understanding of individual learners develop during the lesson?
- Can you predict what a good/average/poor performance or product will look like?
- At which points in the lesson will it be useful for the observers to compare the anticipated behaviours of the pupils against their actual learning behaviours?

The second supervision session (after the first research lesson had been taught) provided opportunities for a discussion of observation data and any other events noticed by pre-service teachers and their mentor. This model of LS which requires focus, prediction and analysis of individual case pupils would encourage and scaffold the development of pre-service students' understanding of classroom practices and interactions as they noticed the connections between what happened during a classroom lesson and the learning of individual pupils. The next set of prompts helped them link the data collected during the first lesson to the revisions needed for the repeat lesson.

- How did your case pupils react to the activities you had planned?
- What evidence do you have which might reveal the development of their understanding of the learning aim?
- Based on this evidence, what kind of adaptions will you make to your original lesson plan when you repeat the lesson?

The prompts in the final supervision session scaffolded pre-service teachers' reflections and challenged them to make connections between their observations to the kinds of lessons they would teach in the future. We hoped our pre-service teachers would be critical of the theories and principles they used as a rationale in their planning and be more able and willing to consider alternative pedagogical alternatives. The differences between what they had noticed during the lessons and what their mentor had noticed could serve to deepen their understanding further. Many students at this stage were of the view that the hard work of a lesson study cycle was now completed. There is a need to make our pre-service students aware that the final supervision session, which proved to be extremely challenging due to its analytical nature, was particularly important in moving them towards level four of the noticing framework. The following prompts below could help them use what they had noticed in a productive and developmental way:

- How close were the predictions of learner behaviours and/or learning to what actually happened?
- What evidence do you have about the way the learners demonstrated their thinking and reasoning during the lesson?
- Did anything noteworthy occur during the lesson that was not predicted?
- Do you have any ideas about why this should be?
- What have you become aware of in the learning of your case pupils?
- To what extent can this be extrapolated to the whole class?

The main aim of the prompts was to encourage pre-service teachers before, during and after practicum to discuss aspects of their teaching at a deeper level. These reflective tools helped them understand the connections between their actions in the classrooms and the opportunities that these actions offer to their pupils' learning. They were able to focus their observations on individual pupils and their learning behaviours at various points during the lesson through the development of their professional noticing skills. In order to scaffold and encourage pre-service teachers to move from a general focus on the whole class in stage one to examining the effects of their teaching on individual pupils in stage four, the prompts that were developed increased in complexity throughout the lesson study cycle.

Examples from the reflective comments written by the pre-service teachers over the last five years revealed that doing LS with the help of prompts increased their knowledge of pupil learning and helped them observe with more focus as they honed their professional noticing skills. Pre-service teachers often said that following the prompts made them more organized and more focused. For example, "I became more focused on pupil responses during the lesson than the lesson mechanics". In addition, this extra focus helped them focus on individual pupils rather than only on the class as a whole. For example, one pre-service teacher wrote, "I now know more about learners' responses and reactions to different teaching approaches". Finally, and perhaps most importantly, one student group wrote, "Throughout our LS, we have realized the different ways of thinking and working that pupils have. Because we have predicted pupils' reactions and then observed them, we have a better idea of what works for this class and why". These reflections provided some evidence that LS with additional prompts was a worthwhile activity for our pre-service teachers to undertake.

## Conclusion

From our point of view as teacher educators and after working with LS for several years, we found that LS supports pre-service teachers' professional development by making them more aware of the relations between their teaching and pupils' learning. We observed that lesson study was challenging for our pre-service teachers and that they needed additional scaffolding to support them in this work. In this chapter, we have introduced two forms of scaffolding tools that pre-service teachers have found useful throughout the LS cycle. The concept of *noticing* has guided our work with these tools. Our aim was to support pre-service teachers in being sensitive to particular aspects of their practices as well as developing the skills for analyzing and inquiring into these aspects.

Working with the *kyouzai kenkyuu* record sheet provided our pre-service teachers with important background knowledge and allowed them to explore potential learning aims and develop well-defined research questions. The record sheet directed the planning, execution and analysis of their research lesson. A deeper understanding of the aims of the lesson also strengthened our pre-service teachers' depth of analysis. The use of *prompts* throughout the LS cycle before, during and after practicum served as reflective tools that helped pre-service teachers build their skills of professional noticing to better understand the connections between their actions in the classrooms and the opportunities that these actions offer to their pupils' learning. These prompts require pre-service teachers to not only describe what they have observed but to dig deeper and make sense of why these pupils reacted in the way they did and to discuss the implications of these for the case pupils, for the class as a whole and for their own professional learning as pre-service teachers.

Working with LS is a learning process for pre-service teachers and for us as teacher educators. We have continued to make improvements to these tools with further feedback from our students since they were first introduced. As we continue our work with LS, new tools are being developed such as audio diaries and summaries. The aim behind all these tools is to ultimately support our pre-service teachers' understanding of the complexities in classrooms so that they can build their classroom skills and deepen their understanding of the connection between teaching and pupil learning. We want them as future teachers to develop their professional noticing to guide and improve teaching in order to support every child's learning.

## Additional readings

Helgevold, N., Naesheim-Bjørkvik, G., & Østrem, S. (2015). Key focus areas and use of tools in mentoring conversations during internship in initial teacher education. *Teaching and Teacher Education*, 49, 128–137.

Mason, J. (2002). *Researching your own practice: The discipline of noticing*. London: Routledge.

Mason, J. (2011). Noticing: Roots and branches. In M. G. Sherin, V. R. Jacobs, & R. A. Philipp (Eds.), *Mathematics teacher noticing: Seeing through teachers' eyes* (pp. 35–50). Studies in Mathematical Thinking and Learning. New York, NY: Routledge.

Naesheim-Bjørkvik, G., Helgevold, N., & Østrem, S. (2019). Lesson study as a professional tool to strengthen collaborative enquiry in mentoring sessions in initial teacher education. *European Journal of Teacher Education*, 42(5), 557–573.

Seleznyov, S. (2016). *Leading lesson study*. London: London Centre for Leadership in Learning.

van Es, E. A. (2011). A framework for learning to notice student thinking. In M. G. Sherin, V. R. Jacobs, & R. A. Philipp (Eds.), *Mathematics teacher noticing: Seeing through teachers' eyes* (pp. 164–181). New York, NY: Routledge.

# 9 Facilitators' roles in lesson study
## From leading the group to doing with the group

*Stéphane Clivaz and Anne Clerc-Georgy*

In Switzerland, little was known about lesson study until the creation of the Lausanne Laboratory Lesson Study (3LS). 3LS was created in 2014 at Lausanne University of Teacher Education (HEP Vaud). Our various experiences of accompanying groups of teachers have allowed us to discover the many facets of the role of the lesson study facilitator. Indeed, we have been led to inhabit different roles related to the different phases of the process. Sometimes it is a matter of introducing participants to the lesson study process, while at other times it is more taking over some organizational tasks. Apart from that, the lesson study facilitator also takes on the role of an expert, the role of a teacher trainer, and even the role of a member of the group.

In this chapter, we will present these different roles as they occur in a lesson study group in mathematics (LSM). The lesson study process was conducted with primary 3 and 4 generalist in-service experienced teachers. The group was composed of eight primary generalist teachers and two facilitators (the two authors of this chapter, a specialist in mathematics didactic and a specialist in teaching and learning). Based on situations and examples drawn from this experience, we will describe these different roles (convenor, teacher trainer, researcher and group member) that were assumed by the facilitators and propose practical guidelines and tips for lesson study facilitators.

### The facilitator's roles

The roles we played as facilitators can be categorized into four aspects: the facilitator as a convenor, as a teacher trainer, as a researcher and as a group member. These roles are not subsequent but often coexist, alternate and influence each other throughout the process. Although they are never clearly separated, we have chosen to treat them one after the other in order to describe them. In our descriptions, you will see at which moment in particular they appeared in the lesson study process supported by one example from the LSM group. We will examine the importance of each of these roles and suggest ideas for developing facilitators of lesson study.

#### The facilitator as a convenor

In Switzerland, as in other countries where lesson study is in its infancy, it is the facilitators who initiate the lesson study process by going to schools to recruit teachers and negotiating with school authorities about the conditions of their participation and arranging the material conditions for the meetings to happen (calendar, room, substitute teachers for research lessons, etc.) with the help of local teachers. The facilitators chair the meetings and make space for everyone to speak but also keep the focus on the subject that is being discussed or point to an idea that could be interesting to discuss. There is evidence in our research that the facilitators steered the discussions to some extent. However, there is also evidence that the other participants also oriented the discussion and that one of the facilitators' important roles when leading the discussion was to keep the conviviality and ensure a climate of trust, as shown in the following exchange.

*Anne*: So, I will ask you a question, in conclusion, about that example. What is the advantage of the decimal system for us?
*Océane*: The regularity. You learn it once, then it's OK!
*Anne*: Yes, for me too, that's the significance of the decimal system, right? That's what the learning of this, is all about. It's what this learning allows us to do. . . . It's interesting that you noted that point!

This role of leading the discussion was even more critical during the moments of synthesis and conclusion in the discussions. During those moments, it was always the role of one of the two facilitators to summarize the discussion. This finalization work was also essential in the elaboration of the students' handouts or of the final lesson plan[1] that had been discussed collaboratively. The choice of leaving this long, quite dull and non-formative task to the facilitators was essentially made to preserve the motivation of the teachers by "assigning it to the ones who were paid to do lesson study". However, the balance between "doing to promote the smooth running of the process" and "not overdoing on behalf of the group members, thus generating passive attitudes in teachers" was challenging to achieve.

---

The balance between being very active in making the meetings as smooth as possible, making sure that everyone's thinking can be safely expressed and making sure that the discussion stays on track is a constant challenge during lesson study meetings. In our experience, having two facilitators who work well together has been a great help and an excellent opportunity to learn about our work as facilitators and, more generally, about our job as educators.

A climate of trust and conviviality is essential in lesson study. Developing this climate cannot be underestimated, and it is more a result of your constant and imperceptible work throughout the meetings. Creating such climate includes fundamental discussion facilitation acts as well as small practical actions.

**Tips for facilitators**

1  Take the time to let the participants get to know each other; allow everyone to express their ideas or observations and to be listened to; do not hesitate to solicit those who speak less; and sometimes bring a box of biscuits!
2  Give directions at the beginning of a discussion and summarize the key points and the decisions taken at the end of it. Keep the discussion on track and monitor the agenda.
3  During the discussion, do not dominate the floor. Sometimes it is useful to talk less so that the discussion can be constructive.

## The facilitator as a teacher trainer

The LSM group that we were involved in was conducted as part of a Continuous Professional Development (CPD) group. The two facilitators are teacher trainers and their university has allocated time for them to conduct CPD. This context necessarily influences and shapes their role in the lesson study process. It positions them as trainers and, as in many CPD contexts, pushes them to lead discussions and provide knowledge to teachers enrolled in training. To avoid misunderstandings, the two facilitators decided to separate their two roles. They agreed in advance to designate one of the two roles as the leader of the discussion for the whole meeting. This role involves ensuring a climate of trust where the facilitator will ask open-ended questions to encourage reflection and allow the expression of essential ideas by the group member in a maieutic aspect. Finally, he/she guides the discussion and ensures that the essential topics mentioned beforehand by the group members are covered. The other facilitator's role is more reserved for most of the meeting. He/she would take notes and participate in the discussion as a group member. Nevertheless, for some parts, he/she might take the position of an expert or a teacher trainer. In the following example, which took place at the end of a long discussion about place value, Anne played the role of conducting the discussion and Stéphane played the role of the expert.

*Caroline*: Seventy and thirty . . . one hundred, it's obvious!
*Anne*: Why is that obvious?
*Valentine*: It's a number bond for ten.
*Caroline*: It's the number bonds for ten, the calculations, the small calculations we know them by heart, it's like multiplication facts, we know them by heart.
*Stéphane*: But why ten, people? [laughs] What is particular about our system is not only that it is ten; it is that the step is the same at all stages. I mean, from one unit to one ten is a factor ten. From one ten to one hundred a factor of ten. From one hundred to one thousand, it's still ten. But not all systems are like that.
*Valentine*: No, there's the binary system.
*Stéphane*: The binary system is by two at a time, but also . . .
*Marie*: There's one interesting thing to do, it's with the hours! . . .
*Stéphane*: That's what's different! It's not so much that it's sixty. It is ten times for hundredths and tenths. From tenths to seconds, it's ten times. Then, from seconds to minutes, it's sixty, then sixty again to hours, then it's twenty-four! And then it's . . .
*A teacher*: It varies!

In the LSM group, the expert role had many facets: a professor answering questions about precise mathematical or pedagogical points, a provider of external resources (research or professional papers, foreign textbooks' tasks, etc.) and a knowledgeable other bringing critical comments at the end of a post lesson discussion. The different kinds of expertise of the two facilitators (teaching and learning for one and mathematics education for the other) helped decide who should be the expert at a precise moment, while the other facilitated the discussion. During the two years, this delineation of the roles became clearer between the two facilitators. As a joint benefit, facilitating the LSM has also encouraged the development of cross-disciplinary expertise among the two facilitators.

> Lesson study in a professional development context, facilitated by teacher trainers, highlights the paradoxes of adult education situations. It is necessary to give directions. Nevertheless, we need to take into account the progress of the group and to allow participants to build knowledge collaboratively while guiding them in this construction without judging their validity. It is equally important to welcome everyone's experiences while providing them with expert knowledge. The balance between these opposing stances is sometimes tricky to find, and it is an ever-changing unstable equilibrium. The challenge is to become and remain an accepted member of the group. Being aware of these tensions and making explicit the different roles of the teacher trainer might help find an adequate balance. Moreover, for teacher trainers, facilitating lesson study might be a way to become more aware of the paradoxes and constraints not only of classroom learning situations but also of adult education situations in other contexts.
>
> **Tips for facilitators**
> 1 Clearly separate the roles of the facilitator and of the teacher trainer or knowledgeable other. If possible, they should be two different persons.
> 2 Make explicit the role you are having at a given moment.

*The facilitator as a researcher*

The facilitator can be a researcher at two levels. At one level, he/she is a member of the group who adopts a research stance in order to solve a teaching and learning problem. The lesson study process aims to have the whole group work on a research lesson. A significant challenge, though, is to encourage the adoption of a researcher's stance by all participants, and the facilitator acts as a role model inviting teachers to become researchers. This was particularly important in earlier LSM cycles. In the following example, the facilitator explained to the group what the research process meant. She pointed out in particular that the solution was not obvious and that it was necessary to risk testing different lessons.

*Anne:* We can also try to improve the lesson because we have identified a number of issues. We will propose a new form of work by modifying more or less the game, more or less the rules, more or less the staging. *We are in a research process*. It means that maybe we'll find that by eliminating issues, we create others that we didn't anticipate. It's part of the process. We're trying things out. We try to solve problems; often when we solve one, we create another. And this is only seen afterwards. It's OK, it's also the approach that requires that. So, we can also take advantage of the fact that we're doing it again to try something different and then compare. Will it really have brought something to help students' learning?

At another level, the facilitator can be an academic researcher studying the lesson study process. It is essential to be aware of the risk of the academic researcher's interests interfering with the interests of lesson study participants. The "meta" perspectives of the facilitator and researcher do not necessarily share the same objectives. On one hand, the facilitator takes a meta look at the lesson study process to ensure that it runs as smoothly as possible. On the other hand, the academic researcher adopts a meta look at the critical aspects of analysis related to the lesson study process. The research questions of the lesson study group and the research questions of the academic researcher are not necessarily the same!

It is important to help teachers to be comfortable with the data collection tools used by researchers such as video recorders. The climate of trust remains crucial, and a letter of consent from participants ensuring teachers' and the pupils' anonymity is needed. This is to assure the teachers that the data collected, particularly the video recordings, will not be used for any type of teacher training purposes. They will only be used for research purposes by the researchers. With these precautions, a climate of confidence and the sense of belonging to a learning community comprising the pupils, teachers, facilitators and researchers can be established. The teachers in our groups always forget the presence of the camera after a few minutes.

---

The facilitator's mission as a researcher is to initiate a research stance in all participants. This stance requires, in particular, openness to different hypotheses and their confrontation with facts and scientific literature. In this role, the facilitator should set aside his or her own research objectives during the lesson study process. The objectives of the research lesson must remain as the focus of attention.

**Tips for facilitators**

1. Do not answer the participants' questions right away. Refer them back to the group.
2. During lesson preparation or debriefing, systematically propose to list several hypotheses.
3. Explore with the group the different hypotheses by referring to observed facts, related knowledge and experience.
4. Compare these observations with some scientific literature.
5. If you are collecting research data about the process, clearly inform the participants about the rules of ethics in a written format.
6. In this case, separate the role of the facilitator from that of the academic researcher. One possibility is to have different persons for these roles. Another option is to wait until the end of the lesson study process to analyze the data.

---

### *The facilitator as a group member*

Being a resource in the lesson study group like any member in the group is a challenge for the facilitators. During earlier LSM meetings, teachers often considered the two facilitators mainly as trainers. Teachers asked the facilitators for advice or knowledge that would allow them to make decisions. The facilitators found themselves in the role of the holder of the solution or truth. Moreover, when the lesson study is organized as part of in-service training, it is normal for teachers to expect facilitators to pass on knowledge to them. In the following example, a teacher challenged the facilitator to provide the "expected answer".

*Anne*:         It's important, because it's really of how things work in real life. . . . What would it be like for you that would justify making a trade before giving the right amount? Or the sum of the points?
*Valentine*:    The learning.
*Anne*:         In what situations? In life?
*Océane*:       When you need change.
*Anne*:         Yeah, why?
                . . .
*Valentine*:    *Give us the answer, you, the pedagogue!*

It takes several cycles for trust to be established and for everyone's expertise to be recognized and assumed. It means that facilitators accept their role as bearers of some types of scientific knowledge. It also means that facilitators accept that their knowledge can be challenged.

In the LSM group, one event particularly helped each participant in the group to feel fully entitled to be a resource: the difficulty in planning and implementing a lesson on problem-solving for which the two facilitators had no preconceived solution. It was in the sharing of a teaching and learning difficulty that allowed the facilitators to position themselves and be fully considered as members of the group. As soon as no participant in the lesson study group had a ready-made answer to offer to the group, all became co-researchers and participants in the co-construction of knowledge.

---

**Tips for facilitators**

Switching from the role of a teacher trainer to that of a member of a group requires:

1   Building mutual trust between facilitators and researchers;
2   Assuming and recognizing one's expertise as well as limitations;
3   Identifying a problem that is a problem for all;
4   Accepting and making it clear that the facilitator may not have the solution to the problem;
5   Allowing each participant to adopt the stance of a researcher.

---

**Training facilitators**

Being an efficient and effective facilitator requires training. This capacity can probably be acquired with experience over time and may include participation in several lesson studies, co-facilitation with experienced colleagues and reading of manuals and literature. However, the specificity of the different roles of a facilitator and the necessity to train more facilitators in schools to ensure the development of lesson studies has led us to develop facilitators' training. Based on our experience and research, such training could include elements about:

1   The history and the particularities of lesson study;
2   Sharing of different lesson study experiences;
3   The different roles and stances of the facilitator in different moments and phases of a lesson study process;

4   The dilemmas and questions that facilitators ask themselves;
5   The relationship between research and lesson study: lesson study as an action-research, use of existing research in lesson study, input of lesson study to academic research and teacher education;
6   The available resources to facilitate lesson study;
7   Observation of a lesson: what to observe and how to make observations productive in a post lesson discussion;
8   The relationship between lesson study and the school as a system.

We believe that such training should articulate inputs from experience and theory and that it should offer practical experiences discussed collectively. We also believe that it should be collaborative and be closely linked to real experiences and lessons that facilitate practice.

**What have we learnt from our experience?**

During our work with the LSM group, the roles of the facilitators were partially implicit in response to the group's expectations and partially explicit as a result of negotiations with the group. The facilitators became more aware of some aspects of these roles along the way as the lesson study process progressed. From our experience of working with several groups and our research data, we came to the conclusion that the negotiations of the roles should be made at several points in the process as these roles evolve. At the beginning of the process, the teacher educators may have to play the roles of convenor, expert and research-stance initiator. This evolution could lead to the roles of convenor being taken over by a teacher of the group. The role of research-stance initiator should also be gradually taken over by a teacher. The facilitators' role can be differentiated from that of a knowledgeable other. The knowledgeable other is usually an expert who intervenes at particular moments in the processes with an external eye on the lesson proposal or on the research lesson, as recommended by Takahashi and McDougal (2016). In our case, some of the teachers participating in our lesson study groups became co-facilitators with us and had increased ownership of the process. Over time, this allowed the "teacher trainer facilitator" to take on the role of a knowledgeable other with a more distant view of the process, making the lesson study more sustainable.

Another aspect in our practice is the participation of two facilitators with different and complementary kinds of expertise. It enabled us to alternate among the roles of a group leader, an observer of the process and an expert. It was an opportunity for us to learn from each other as well as from the participating teachers, and we have learnt a lot in the process as facilitators.

*Anne:*   I learn, I learn when I'm with you, I learn, and it's fabulous, at all levels. . . . Besides, I enjoy tremendously working here, discussing my notes again. It's a little more selfish, but I feel like I'm learning with you both mathematically and in terms of the connection to the classroom. And for a teacher educator, it's just magical and generous of you to grant us access to the questions you ask yourself, the problems you face. And then, of course, it shakes my conceptions and what I say to student teachers. . . . It puts me in a lot of doubt. It makes me progress a lot, and I have this feeling as much when I observe myself as when I observe the group. . . . It's amazing how much we see ourselves moving forward. We see ourselves progressing. We see ourselves transforming. . . . I come out energized of every single session we've had. And full of questions. Always.

## Conclusion

In this chapter, we have highlighted the complex interplay of the facilitator's roles as a convenor, as a teacher trainer, as a researcher and as a group member. We drew from our own experience as facilitators with several lesson study groups as well as the analysis of our roles and stances. We have also relied on the points of view of other lesson study facilitators, experts and researchers from all over the world. The dynamic of the international aspect and the very local aspect of lesson study has been a great inspiration in our Swiss experience.

## Note

1 The four lesson plans produced by this group are available on the 3LS website: www.hepl.ch/3LS.

## Additional readings

Baetschmann, K., Balegno, M., Baud, E., Chevalley, M., Clerc-Georgy, A., Clivaz, S., & Weber, A. (2015). Une expérience de lesson study en mathématiques en 5–6 Harmos [A Lesson study experience in mathematics for grade 3–4]. *L'éducateur*, (11), 32–34. Retrieved from www.hepl.ch/files/live/sites/systemsite/files/laboratoire_3ls/EducateurLessonStudy11_2015.pdf

Batteau, V., & Clivaz, S. (2016). Le dispositif de formation continue lesson study: travail autour d'une leçon de numération [Lesson study as a professional development setting: A lesson about place value]. *Grand N*, *98*, 27–48.

Clerc-Georgy, A., & Clivaz, S. (2016). Evolution des rôles entre chercheurs et enseignants dans un processus lesson study: quel partage des savoirs? In F. Ligozat, M. Charmillot, & A. Muller (Eds.), *Le partage des savoirs dans les processus de recherche en éducation* (pp. 189–208). Série Raisons Educatives, No. 20. Brussels: De Boeck.

Clivaz, S. (2015). Les Lesson Study: Des situations scolaires aux situations d'apprentissage professionnel pour les enseignants. [Lessons study: From school situations to professional learning situations for teachers]. *Revue des HEP et institutions assimilées de Suisse romande et du Tessin*, *19*, 99–105. Retrieved from www.revuedeshep.ch/site-fpeq-n/Site_FPEQ/19_files/2015-Clivaz-FPEQ-19.pdf

Clivaz, S. (2016). Lesson study: From professional development to research in mathematics education. *Quadrante*, *25*(1), 97–112. Retrieved from www.apm.pt/portal/quadrante.php?id=223147&rid=223131

Clivaz, S. (2018). Développement des connaissances mathématiques pour l'enseignement au cours d'un processus de lesson study. In T. Barrier & C. Chambris (Eds.), *Actes du séminaire national de didactique des mathématiques 2016* (pp. 287–302). Paris: IREM de Paris–Université Paris Diderot.

Clivaz, S., Clerc-Georgy, A., & Batteau, V. (2016). Lesson study en mathématiques: un dispositif japonais de développement professionnel des enseignants à l'épreuve du contexte suisse-romand. In Y. Matheron & G. Gueudet (Eds.), *Actes de la 18e école d'été de didactique des mathématiques* (pp. 487–502). Grenoble: La Pensée Sauvage.

Clivaz, S., & Ni Shuilleabhain, A. (2019). What knowledge do teachers use in lesson study? A focus on mathematical knowledge for teaching and levels of teacher activity. In R. Huang, A. Takahashi, & J. P. da Ponte (Eds.), *Theory and practice of lesson study in mathematics: An international perspective* (pp. 419–440). Cham: Springer International.

Martin, D., & Clerc-Georgy, A. (2017). La lesson study, une démarche de recherche collaborative en formation des enseignants? *Phronesis*, *6*(1–2), 47. Retrieved from www.cairn.info/revue-phronesis-2017-1-page-35.htm

Ni Shuilleabhain, A., & Clivaz, S. (2017). Analyzing teacher learning in lesson study: Mathematical knowledge for teaching and levels of teacher activity. *Quadrante*, *26*(2), 99–125. Retrieved from https://researchrepository.ucd.ie/handle/10197/9695

Takahashi, A., & McDougal, T. (2016). Collaborative lesson research: Maximizing the impact of lesson study. *ZDM*, *48*(4), 1–14. https://doi.org/10.1007/s11858-015-0752-x

# 10 Facilitating a lesson study team to adopt an inquiry stance

*Siebrich de Vries and Iris Uffen*

## Introduction

A successful ingredient in lesson study is the adoption of an inquiry stance among teachers in their lesson study cycles. An inquiry stance is an open and critical way of looking, aimed at deeper insights. Teachers with an inquiry stance show an open attitude: they are curious and critical, they want to understand and they are willing to change perspectives. They are also willing to distance themselves from their own routines. They focus on resource use and like to work conscientiously and effectively. Moreover, they like to share the insights they have gained with others.

Teachers need to adopt an inquiry stance in lesson study because lesson study is classroom research. Lesson study first begins with the teacher's own learning question(s) and they then search for a common research question among members of their team. They will answer this research question by building and refining their ideas about teaching and learning through careful, collaborative study of resources and actual instruction. In so doing, they become more aware of their *practical knowledge*, and they will adjust it if necessary. We understand *practical knowledge* as all kinds of knowledge and beliefs about teaching and learning that teachers individually and often unconsciously develop through their experience, and how that influences and drives their actions in the classroom.

---

An inquiry stance is an open and critical way of looking, aimed at deeper insight.

A teacher who has an inquiry stance will:

instead of prejudices, have an open mind;
instead of being uninterested, be curious;
instead of taking everything for granted, have a critical mind;
instead of being satisfied quickly, want to understand;
instead of sticking to his own point of view, be willing to switch perspectives;
instead of sticking to his/her own routines, distance himself/herself from them;
instead of using no resources, want to build on previous views and ideas;
instead of sloppy work, focus on accuracy;
instead of keeping gained insights to himself, like to share them with others.

---

*Figure 10.1* Characteristics of an inquiry stance

Source: Based on Bruggink and Harinck (2012).

In this chapter, we will first explain that teachers with an inquiry stance predominantly practise what is called *exploratory talk* in their lesson studies, and then we will describe the kinds of potential results that may occur. Second, we will discuss why teachers often have challenges in trying to adopt this stance. Third, we will discuss how important it is for teams who are not familiar with lesson study to have a facilitator. We will discuss the two roles that facilitators will need to play in supporting teachers to adopt an inquiry stance and will conclude our discussion of each role with suggestions of what facilitators can do.

## Conversations in the lesson study team

In conversations in which an inquiry stance is visible, teachers predominantly practise what is called *exploratory talk* (see Figure 10.2). During the exploration, teachers look for a deeper and shared understanding of (the) potential answer(s) to the research question(s) that guide(s) their lesson study. They play the role of a critical friend to deepen the conversation, for example by expressing a doubt or wonder and asking each other critical questions. They also make explicit their thinking and explain their ideas with theories from curriculum and subject matter, pedagogy and educational science or from their observations of students during the research lesson. The focus of lesson study team conversations should be on student learning, and teachers would need to look for how subject matter and pedagogy intersects with their learning.

In exploratory conversations, teachers develop new knowledge and insights. They sincerely want to understand and listen to each other freely without prejudice and without trying to influence each other, and without clinging to or defending of own ideas. When teachers are able to "problematize" their own teaching practice, to question their established routines and beliefs about learning and teaching, and are open to understand the views of colleagues, they are better able to change their attitudes and accept new knowledge and practices.

The new practical knowledge that a team constructs in this way is no longer personal and unconscious but becomes joint and explicit. Lesson study teachers do this through social interaction and critical reflection and by experimenting in the research lesson and integration of the theory. Theory is often separate from the work of the teacher in the classroom and is therefore hardly applicable, but in the lesson study process, teachers connect theory and practice very easily and almost automatically. This narrows the "eternal" gap between theory

---

**Exploratory talk**
Teachers engage critically but constructively with each other's ideas. Statements and suggestions are offered for joint consideration. These may be challenged and counter-challenged, but challenges are justified, and alternative hypothesis are offered. Compared with cumulative talk, in exploratory talk knowledge is made more publicly accountable and reasoning is more visible in the talk.

**Cumulative talk**
Teachers build positively but uncritically on what the other has said. Teachers use talk to construct a 'common knowledge' by accumulation. Repetitions, confirmations, and elaborations characterize cumulative discourse.

---

*Figure 10.2* Characteristics of exploratory talk versus cumulative talk

Source: Based on Mercer and Littleton (2007).

and practice (see Figure 10.3). They integrate the new practical knowledge that the lesson study process has developed into their own practice. In this way, they are able to develop professionally and improve their teaching in the classroom.

## Challenges in adopting an inquiry stance

It is the experience of many lesson study teams that the adoption of an inquiry stance appears to be difficult. We have noticed conversations that are predominantly qualifying and cumulative instead of being joint and explorative (see Figure 10.2). In such conversations, topics are discussed in descriptive ways in terms of "who did or said what?" Often a non-substantiated value judgement is given. Team members do not respond substantively to what the other person says. Instead they add even more descriptive, anecdotal information or introduce a new topic (see Figure 10.4 for examples). The underlying reasons for this could be at an individual, team and/or organizational level.

On an individual level, too little knowledge of and experience with joint exploration makes teachers uncertain or nervous, thereby provoking feelings of resistance. This also applies if

---

In the lesson study process, teachers have to get ideas and new perspectives on how to interpret and improve student learning on a specific topic. For this purpose:

- they can talk to experts and invite them to a meeting;
- they can also study (scientific) journal articles, (study) books, and if available, national curriculum guidelines or other resources. The facilitator can help to find suitable resources.

In the planning stage, teachers incorporate the ideas heard from the experts or found in the theory in their lesson plan.

During the research lesson, the teacher giving the research lesson can safely try out the ideas, and the other team members can observe how the ideas affect students.

In this way, teachers apply theory into the lesson study practice. The result may be that they adjust their beliefs and teaching behaviour or even arrive at new beliefs and new teaching behaviour in their own individual teaching practice.

---

*Figure 10.3* Connecting theory and practice

---

Teacher A: '*The students were not paying attention in the beginning of the lesson. I think the introduction was too long and too boring. We should shorten the introduction and maybe show only the video clip.*'

Teacher B: '*The students did learn a lot, they were so enthusiastic. You could see their engagement, especially when they had to solve the puzzle with their neighbours. It worked out for them. We should keep this in the lesson.*'

Teacher C: '*I think the scheme was too difficult to use as a resource for the students. You could see the frustration; they did not get it at all. They did not even get it after they tried to explain it to each other. I think we should offer them something else.*'

---

*Figure 10.4* Individual utterances that show lack of exploration

they are not sufficiently familiar with lesson study or with the chosen theme, or if they have not yet experienced the added value of lesson study or the chosen theme.

At the team level, teachers are expected to work closely together in an area that they almost always approach individually: the students in the classroom. Teachers may find this collaboration difficult because it comes not without obligations. In addition, they face different perspectives and opinions which may be uncomfortable for some. There can be a perception that the other is non-receptive and biased, although often this is due to inconsistencies in ideas that people may have. Bohm (2004) calls these "blockades", which people (unconsciously) prefer to maintain in order to not disturb their own peace of mind.

Both at team level and at organizational level, the established standards and ways of communication do not necessarily support an inquiry stance. At times, they even complicate it. For example, it may not be common at school to talk to colleagues about their own teaching practice. How colleagues view lesson study could also affect teachers' own stance towards lesson study. A facilitator can provide support if a lesson study team does not show exploratory talk for any reason.

## The lesson study facilitator: two roles to develop an inquiry stance

Every lesson study team and every lesson study is different, and this requires a facilitator to continuously interpret the process and adjust if necessary. At times, a facilitator may experience stagnation in the lesson study process without knowing the underlying reasons. In response to this variety and uncertainty, the following sections will discuss the basis of the two roles and suggest some possibilities for a facilitator to stimulate a (starting) team to develop an inquiry stance by first creating a safe climate and then by guiding participants through the process.

## Creating a safe climate

The focus of a lesson study cycle lies in searching for an answer to the research question. The aim is to better understand different perspectives towards this research question from colleagues in the lesson study team, professional and research literature, and possibly external experts. The perspectives gained from the data collected during the research lesson also provide invaluable inputs in the process. An important condition for this process to succeed is a safe climate and mutual trust among members of the team.

### *Building mutual trust*

The facilitator can increase the mutual trust of the team members by paying attention to their getting to know each other. They can hold a conversation about a good lesson they had recently taught and share their views, expectations and goals they may have in collaborating with colleagues in lesson study. One way to achieve this is to prepare a protocol with group norms (see Figure 10.5) and to state explicitly the norms of collaboration at each meeting.

### *Provide information about the nature of lesson study*

Unfamiliarity with lesson study and its nature can cause uncertainty. One way to respond to this is to provide information about exploratory ways of talking and other aspects of lesson study. The facilitator can for example discuss the characteristics of an inquiry stance (see Figure 10.1), the characteristics of exploratory talk versus qualifying and cumulative talk (see

Figure 10.2) and the basic ground rules of exploratory conversations (see Figure 10.6). It is also important for the facilitator to be a role model. Through this, the team members will know how to make their own perspectives explicit and see for themselves how perspectives can change during their discussion. As these (mutual) expectations become clearer, a safer and a more productive collaboration can arise.

## *Make communication itself the subject of conversation*

It would be helpful if the facilitator makes it a practice to speak about team communication on a regular basis and provide feedback. This could prevent future communication problems that could occur within the team. If such practice is not the norm, it would be difficult to address such communications problems when they arise.

The facilitator could address the following agenda at meetings on several levels, for example, (1) *topics*: what teachers will discuss; (2) *procedures*: how is the meeting to be structured and what lesson study specific tasks are going to be performed; (3) *interaction*: how should teachers talk to each other; and (4) *experiences/feelings*: what (un)comfortable experiences are needed to be addressed to ensure smooth progress of the collaboration. In Figure 10.7, we offer a method on how to discuss the subject of communication during a lesson study meeting using a plan-do-check-adjust-cycle (PDCA-cycle), which is an iterative cycle to ensure continuous improvement by planning what to improve (plan), doing what is planned (do), checking if the plan worked and why (check) and lastly by formulating what to do in the future (adjust).

---

1. Think individually:

   ✓ What do you expect from the collaboration?
   ✓ What do you need to work well together?
   ✓ How do you want to deal with any disagreement?
   ✓ What do you need to develop yourself?
   ✓ What do you experience as an obstacle in the process?

2. Discuss and write down together:

   ✓ What agreements about our collaboration do we want to develop for our lesson study process?
   ✓ How do we want to deal with these agreements about our collaboration during the lesson study process?

---

*Figure 10.5* Helpful questions in preparation for the group protocol

---

✓ We invite everybody to speak
✓ We will respect each other's input
✓ We will actively listen to each other
✓ We will repeatedly clarify our understanding of what other team members are saying
✓ We will respect and value tentative ideas
✓ We will give and ask for reasons and alternative explanations
✓ We will share what we do know, and what we do *not* know
✓ We will make a group decision after considering alternative explanations.

---

*Figure 10.6* Basic ground rules of exploratory conversations

Source: Based on Littleton and Mercer (2013).

*Take resistance seriously*

If the facilitator detects resistance within the team, the general advice is to take this seriously and discuss this resistance openly. This may help to lower resistance and help increase the feeling of safety (see Figure 10.8).

| Activity | When | Questions |
|---|---|---|
| **Plan** | Beginning of every meeting | What (topics) are we going to talk about?<br>What are the (lesson study) procedures during this meeting?<br>What are important goals for our interaction?<br>What do we expect from each other?<br>Is anyone experiencing/feeling something now or earlier that we may have missed which we can address?<br>How do we take this into account? |
| **Do** | During every meeting | Execute what is planned. |
| **Check** | End of every meeting | How did it go regarding…<br>… what (topics) we have discussed?<br>… the (lesson study) procedures?<br>… our interaction?<br>… our experiences/feelings? |
| **Adjust** | End of every meeting | What did we learn from our check?<br>How do we take these into account for subsequent meetings? |

*Figure 10.7* Helpful questions for discussing the communication in the lesson study team

- ✓ **Build mutual trust** by paying attention to getting to know each other; for example:
    - hold a conversation about a recent lesson which teachers are happy about;
    - hold a conversation about the views, expectations and goals teachers have for their lesson study;
    - prepare a group protocol with common work and behavioural agreements (see Figure 10.5), and put these agreements on the agenda of each meeting.

- ✓ **Provide information about the collaborative and exploratory nature of lesson study**, for example:
    - discuss the characteristics of an inquiry stance (see Figure 10.1);
    - discuss the characteristics of exploratory talk versus cumulative talk (see Figure 10.2);
    - discuss the basic ground rules of exploratory conversations (see Figure 10.6);
    - be a role model yourself and try to deepen:
        - "Is good enough OK for your students?"
        - "Does "good enough "encourage all your students to learn?"
        - "How can we make this lesson as good as possible for every student?"
    or ask further questions:
        - "What would happen if …?"
        - "How would X be different if …?"
        - "What is another way to …?"
        - "Why do you think …?"

- ✓ **Make communication itself the subject of conversation** (see Figure 10.7)

- ✓ **Take resistance seriously**

*Figure 10.8* Summarized suggestions for a facilitator to support teachers to adopt an inquiry stance by creating a safe climate

## Guiding participants through the process

It is not immediately clear to each teacher what is the usefulness of the different stages of a lesson study cycle and how to go through the various processes involved. Starting teams, for example, often focus more on the product, which is to develop a lesson plan, rather than on the process. There is a tendency to focus more on the creation of the most perfect lesson possible rather than on the effects on student learning or ones' own learning (Lewis, 2016). The facilitator will need to stimulate the inquiry stance in different ways while guiding the team through the process.

### *Pay explicit attention to the purpose of lesson study and its stages*

One way to help teachers understand and value the process is for the facilitator to pay explicit and repeated attention to generating awareness among teachers of the purpose of lesson study and the way in which the various components and stages can contribute to their professional development and learning. It is important for a facilitator to not only know lesson study well but also to understand a key idea behind lesson study, which is about teachers working collaboratively and systematically to improve the quality of their own teaching practice.

### *Check whether explicit attention should be paid to research skills*

In addition, it may be useful to check whether explicit attention should be paid to research skills, such as performing a problem analysis, formulating a good research question, designing a research lesson, collecting data (in particular through observation and interviewing), analyzing data and interpreting results. Such research processes are not in the daily routine of many teachers. Guiding the formulation of a research question deserves special attention because it will drive all subsequent meetings and lay the foundation for the entire lesson study cycle.

### *Help to formulate the research question*

The facilitator can help to identify which problems or (learning) questions one has about student learning or what the teachers wonder about in their own lessons. In Figure 10.9, we describe a method, the goal system interview, which the supervisor can use to uncover teachers' learning questions in a lesson study. The topics discussed are then processed into a common research question that all team members consider to be both interesting and relevant to investigate for their own teaching. It is important that the research question is focused on student learning and that the concepts used can also be made visible during the research lesson so that they are observable (see Figure 10.10 for ingredients for the research question). The facilitator strives for consensus within the team and encourages everyone to feel ownership of the process. This can increase cohesion and joint purpose, which can benefit the will and the ability to adopt an inquiry stance.

### *Make explicit underlying assumptions*

For the purpose of exploratory talk, in which teachers make explicit their (unconscious) practical knowledge including underlying assumptions, the facilitator can help teachers by investigating cases through a critical reflective dialogue (see Figure 10.11). However, the facilitator must realize that making underlying thinking patterns visible within a team in the context of a lesson study will take extra time but that it will be worth the time invested.

Finding out one's learning questions, starts by mapping out what a teacher usually does and why he thinks this is important. This could be clearly and compactly displayed in a goal system. A goal system can easily be constructed on the basis of an interview. Teachers of the lesson study team could interview each other to map out each other's goal system. For an interview you only need an A3 paper and a stack of post-it leaflets. The interview is as follows:

1.
The interviewing teacher asks the other teacher to consider a recent lesson and asks the following question: *What did you do successfully in the lesson?* The interviewing teacher writes each part of a lesson on a separate post-it sheet, in the words of the other teacher

2.
The interviewing teacher asks the question for each lesson part: *Why do you think this is important?* These answers (goals) should be written on post-it sheets and pasted onto the A3 sheet. A lesson component could contribute to multiple goals. These relationships between goals and means are represented by connecting with an arrow the lesson component to one (or more) goal(s). For each goal, the interviewer asks why the teacher considers this goal important, until the teacher has 'arrived' at his most important goals for teaching.

3.
Finally, the interviewing teacher asks the other teacher to evaluate his goal system based on the following question: Which goals are you satisfied with and which goals are you less satisfied with? The colour white is used to identify a satisfied goal and a grey color is used to identify a less satisfied goal.

Through this process, the teachers of a lesson study team will be able to discover their learning questions that can drive their search for a common research question.

An example of a goal system of biology teacher, Ilse:

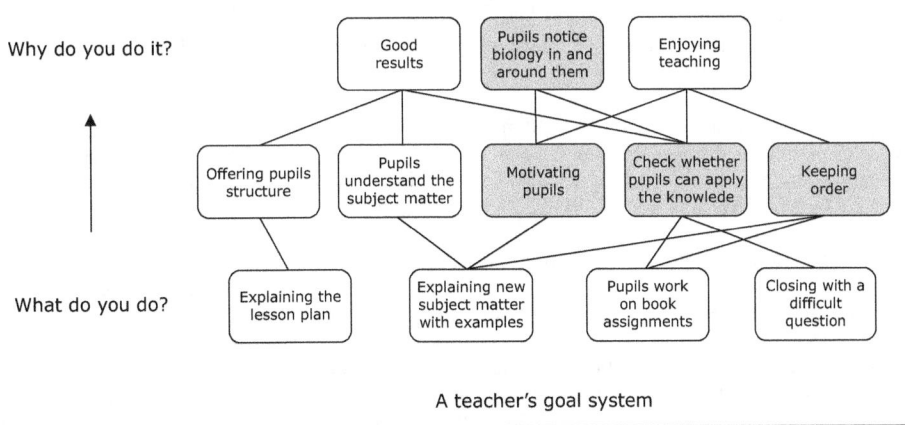

*Figure 10.9* A goal system interview

Source: Based on Janssen, Gradstein, Nobels, and Van Bemmel (n.d.).

**Do's:**
- ✓ Relevant for the daily practice of all team members
- ✓ Starting the question with 'how': *how* will students learn during the research lesson that will contribute to achieving the learning objective?
- ✓ Using concepts that are clear and can be made observable

**Don'ts:**
- ✓ Interesting for all the team members, but not relevant for their daily practice
- ✓ Starting the question with 'do' or 'to what extent': to what extent did students learn during the research lesson?
- ✓ Using concepts that are vague and too complex to be made observable

**Examples**

How do students learn to make sense of their own and others' underlying values when discussing moral dilemmas with fellow students?

How do students learn the meaning and correct use of *mol* when we provide different resources students can consult when learning this?

How does learning about the system of a language contributes to the understanding and correct use of the present perfect?

*Figure 10.10* Ingredients for the research question

Step 1: Choosing a theme (10 minutes)
Each teacher submits a pedagogical or didactical question or case. The group then decides which theme to work with.

Step 2: Exploring each other's views (15 minutes)
Each teacher answers the question: How would I (pedagogically or didactically) act in this situation and what are my motives?

Step 3: Talk about each other's views (30 minutes)
The teachers then discuss the views, positions and ideas, a possible approach, the possible dilemmas, bottlenecks, the outcome, etc. They do this by asking the same question five times, starting with WHAT, WHY, FOR WHAT PURPOSE and HOW.

Step 4: Back to the theme (20 minutes)
What did I discover after talking about each other's views? What is the significance of the discovery in my view? What does that mean for my pedagogical or didactical actions?

Step 5: Reflection on the critical reflexive dialogue (10 minutes)
Teachers talk to each other about the critical reflexive dialogue as an aid in exploring, deepening and investigating their own and each other's underlying views of pedagogical and/or didactical action.

*Figure 10.11* Critical reflective dialogue

Source: Based on Kessels, Boers, and Mostert (2008).

### *Stimulate depth by modelling exploratory talk*

When teachers find it difficult to ask each other self-directed exploratory questions, the facilitator can play a key role in modelling exploratory talk. One way is by structuring the conversation at any point by sharing what is expected from the teachers. Another way is to ask questions that will provoke exploratory talk. This requires a thorough understanding by the facilitator of what it means to talk in an exploratory way, as the facilitator could easily steer the conversation in a non-explorative direction. In the example in Figure 10.12, we show how a facilitator models the conversation by structuring and asking questions. To demonstrate more clearly the influence of the facilitator at different levels, we put cumulative talk and exploratory talk side by side.

### *Redirect deficit thinking by conversational moves*

Another way of role modelling by a facilitator is through conversational moves. One such move involves reframing deficit thinking about students. If a teacher, for example, expresses concern or frustration about "low achieving students" or attributes low academic performance to ability or motivation, the facilitator can redirect the conversation to highlight the specific learning skills that the students exhibit (Park, 2018, p. 635). In this way, the facilitator

---

Teacher A: "I am not sure whether student A did learn. This is what he said: '*their* bike, is written as '*there* bike, right?' The other students responded 'yes, yes, that is true.' And they kept on confirming each other's input like this, and I was sitting there like… yeah… what to think. And then something struck student A. He corrected himself and said 'their bike… you write *their*'. But how come he said so? Because the group next to them was telling that 'their' was the right way to spell 'their' in this sentence. So long story short, I am not sure what student A did learn about this specific grammar rule. He got it right, but did he learn?"

| **Example of qualifying or cumulative talk** | **Modelling exploratory talk** |
|---|---|
| Facilitator: "Well that is difficult to answer, as the goal of the lesson could also be formulated better. Let's move on, I would like to hear everyone's observations." | Facilitator: "You are not sure whether the student did learn based on the observations you just shared. Our research question is how students learn grammar rules in collaboration with fellow students and with the help of the grammar tool you as a team developed. |
| Teacher B: "I observed student B, and he was behaving as we expected. Doing his best, paying attention, collaborating with his team mates. Yes, I think he did a great job, he had no difficulties with this assignment." | So, this question you raise is key in answering our research question. Before we move on to the other team members' observations, let's make sure we know what you observed and let's interpret together the meaning of your observations for our research question. Do you [team members] have questions for teacher A? What do you need to know from her observations to get a grip on how student A learned grammar rules during the research lesson?" |
| Facilitator: "So you think the lesson was successful for student B?" | |
| Teacher B: "Yes, he definitely reached the goal of the lesson." | |
| Facilitator: "Great, nice to observe. Thank you for sharing. Teacher C, what did you observe?" | |

*Figure 10.12* Stimulating depth by modelling exploratory talk

> 1. Implications for teachers' own teaching practice
> 2. Learning about one's own learning process
> 3. The collaboration and inquiry stance during lesson study
> 4. Dissemination of learning outcomes
> 5. A look ahead: which follow-up questions are important and which improvements are recommended for the next lesson study cycle

*Figure 10.13* Themes for reflection and consolidation

stimulates teachers to start thinking about what students are able to do and help them develop further instead of what they are not good at. Conversational moves enacted within lesson study meetings can move teams towards an inquiry stance and an asset-based approach to student learning.

*Stimulate reflection and consolidation*

To encourage reflection and the consolidation of what has been learned during the process, a facilitator can encourage the team to document ideas, thoughts, decisions and lessons learned. Ways of doing that include keeping a log or by closing each meeting with Google Forms and occasionally reviewing them when needed, for example, when preparing for a post lesson discussion of a research lesson. Looking back and reflecting is necessary to move from experience to knowledge. This can be further encouraged by asking the team at the end of the cycle to show their thinking and learning process by producing a "product". This could be a report, a presentation or an article for a journal. Suggestions for themes to discuss during reflection are shown in Figure 10.13.

*Develop the team's self-reliance*

As teams better understand lesson study and develop their inquiry stance, the facilitator can progressively reduce his/her role. The facilitator can discuss with the team what different tasks and roles the facilitator has had during the lesson study cycle and which of these tasks or roles can be gradually taken over by the team. For example, one of the team members can take the lead in monitoring the formulation of the research question. Another team member can monitor if different perspectives are adequately addressed and explored during the lesson study process (see Figure 10.14).

## Conclusion

In this chapter, we have illustrated that a facilitator can play a useful role in lesson study teams with teachers who have little experience with an inquiry stance. There are two roles for facilitators to play: first, by creating a safe climate, and second, by guiding participants through the process. We have provided examples of how these roles can be performed by the facilitator during lesson study to promote the inquiry stance of teachers in a lesson study team. Teachers will ultimately be better able to develop professionally and improve their teaching in the classroom if they are given support from facilitators.

- ✓ **Pay explicit attention to the purpose of lesson study and its stages:**
  - make the purpose of each stage explicit, and check its understanding;
  - keep the focus of the lesson study stage / conversations;
  - ensure that all participants are involved and contribute, listen to each other, build on each other's ideas.

  If necessary:
  - stop the process and agree with the group how it is going and how to proceed;
  - spend more or less time on a particular step, or change the order of the steps.

  Advice to always discuss these actions with the team and to substantiate them.

- ✓ **Check whether explicit attention should be paid to research skills**, such as
  - performing a problem analysis;
  - formulating a good research question;
  - designing a research lesson;
  - collecting data (in particular through observation and interviewing);
  - analyzing data and interpreting results.

- ✓ **Help to formulate the research question** (see Figures 10.9 and 10.10)

- ✓ **Help participants make explicit their (unconscious) practical knowledge** (see Figure 10.11)

- ✓ **Stimulate depth by modeling exploratory talk** (see Figure 10.12)

- ✓ **Redirect deficit thinking by conversational moves**

- ✓ **Stimulate reflection and consolidation** (see Figure 10.13)

- ✓ **Develop the team's self-reliance,** by progressively reducing the facilitator's role.

*Figure 10.14* Summarized suggestions for a facilitator to support teachers to adopt an inquiry stance by guiding participants through the process

## Additional readings

Bohm, D. (2004). *On dialogue*. New York, NY: Routledge (Original work published 1996).
Bruggink, M., & Harinck, F. (2012). De onderzoekende houding van leraren: wat wordt daaronder verstaan? [The inquiry stance of teachers: What is meant by that?] *Tijdschrift voor lerarenopleiders (VELON/VELON), 33*(3), 46–53.
Janssen, F.J.J.M., Gradstein, O., Nobels, J., & Van Bemmel, H. (n.d.). *Toolkit practical differentiation*. Retrieved from www.talenteducation.eu/toolkitforteachers/practicaldifferentiation/en/
Janssen, F.J.J.M., Westbroek, H. B., Doyle, W., & Van Driel, J. H. (2013). How to make innovation practical. *Teachers College Record, 115*(7), 1–43.
Kessels, J., Boers, E., & Mostert, P. (2008). *Vrije ruimte praktijkboek, Filosoferen in Organisaties* [Free space practice book: Philosophizing in organisations]. Amsterdam: Boom.
Lewis, J. M. (2016). Learning to lead, leading to learn: How facilitators learn to lead lesson study. *ZDM, 48*(4), 527–540.
Littleton, K., & Mercer, N. (2013). *Interthinking: Putting talk to work*. London: Routledge.
Mercer, N., & Littleton, K. (2007). *Dialogue and the development of children's thinking*. London: Routledge.
Park, V. (2018). Leading data conversation moves: Toward data-informed leadership for equity and learning. *Educational Administration Quarterly, 54*(4), 617–647.

# 11 Learner-centered facilitation in lesson study groups

*Shannon Morago and Sveva Grigioni Baur*

In this chapter, we introduce the idea of learner-centered facilitation and how it supports lesson study groups to develop a more in-depth understanding of how to meet student needs. By presenting a case of cross-cultural pre-service teachers engaging in lesson study, we illustrate the process of learner-centered facilitation and how it can result in a deeper knowledge in teachers of not only effective ways to meet student learning needs but also how to trust and guide their own students through productive struggle. The examples of the approach, as well as the facilitation guidelines, will provide information on the mindset and skills needed to implement learner-centered facilitation, including direction on how to resolve critical situations that can arise while facilitating an LS group.

## Learner-centered facilitation

Learner-centered facilitation is a method of guiding lesson study groups that assumes teachers will develop new learning about pupils, effective teaching, and collaboration when they use and confront their pre-existing ideas and are provided opportunities and experiences to gather evidence about what works to develop student understanding. This type of facilitation allows struggle and trusts that teachers will develop the necessary knowledge, skills and dispositions when confronted with evidence of their decisions. Through the use of group norming, guiding and reflective questions and tasks, and the expectation that decisions should be made with consensus and data, learner-centered facilitation pushes groups to trust and test their decision-making process in terms of what is best for pupil learning (see Figure 11.1). It goes beyond the idea of learning new ways to teach; it also pushes teachers to construct and use a process for analyzing their own teaching and engaging with their students.

Like classroom teachers, lesson study (LS) facilitators choose their facilitation style based on their beliefs about how people learn. When a facilitator is guiding a group towards an outcome, they choose strategies they think are most likely to result in the outcome being attained. Some teachers believe that learners need to be directly given information to understand and that to motivate learners there should be positive and negative reinforcement. Some teachers have a more constructivist-based stance and believe that designing tasks that allow learners to build their understanding, and to explore and engage with content in a collaborative environment, is key. We are teachers and teacher educators who facilitate from the principles of the second, constructivist-based approach. We believe that elements of this approach, such as providing opportunities for teachers to actively consider and construct meaning through authentic experiences and in collaboration with others, are important for developing the knowledge, skills, and dispositions that underly effective teaching. Our facilitation model is developed from this foundation and these beliefs.

| |
|---|
| What learner-centered facilitation is and isn't* <br> (*adapted from the chapter format in Johnson, Perez and Uline 2013) |
| What Learner-centered Facilitation *is* <br> • Provides a secure space that allows open-minded discussions between teachers <br> • Upholds the sharing of ideas between group members <br> • Requires facilitator(s) to <br>   - listen carefully during group discussions to understand specific group needs <br>   - develop and ask questions, promoting metacognition and discussion between teachers, including seeking data from pupils to make decisions <br>   - uphold deep understanding about teaching/learning skills and dispositions <br>   - uphold deep understanding about how children learn <br>   - allow teachers to find specific solutions to teaching challenges <br>   - trust the process of teachers constructing their understanding through a productive and guided struggle |
| What the learner-centered facilitation *isn't* <br> • Providing answers <br> • Providing best-practices tips <br> • Defining what is right or wrong <br> • Allowing teachers to make thoughtless decisions <br> • To showcase the expertise of facilitators |

*Figure 11.1* What learner-centered facilitation is and isn't

In our experience, novice teachers often want to be shown and told how to proceed, how to teach, how to solve a problem, or that they are doing something correctly. They trust us as facilitators and want to hear that what they are doing is right, often because they lack an understanding of whether something works. Telling them takes the learning (and responsibility) out of their hands and removes opportunities for them to develop understanding through cause and effect. In contrast, learner-centered facilitation places the responsibility for learning on the teachers. It also requires a facilitator's trust that the teacher will build the necessary mental framework or mindset related to effective teaching and pupil learning.

To do this, facilitators must first believe that learning will occur when teachers struggle, collaborate, and follow the process. Being thoughtful about how the teachers are learning, taking time before responding to participant questions, planning for and using reflective questions rather than suggestions, tips or advice about how to proceed, are all methods of maintaining a learner-centered facilitation approach.

## Background of the case: development of learner-centered facilitation

In order to better introduce the role of facilitator as we have experienced it, we will present a case of cross-cultural pre-service teachers engaging in lesson study that we co-facilitated. This allows us not only to highlight key factors of its implementation but also shows the effects of this type of facilitation. Moreover, engaging with a real situation proves that facilitation is a practical act and not just a theoretical concept.

Our approach was developed over eight years of facilitating seven international and cross-cultural lesson study groups (Groups 1–7) comprising pre-service science and math teachers. Each year, three students from a teacher training institute in Switzerland and three undergraduates interested in teaching from a public university in Northern California were placed in a lesson study group for ten months. During this time the six pre-service teachers collaboratively developed a lesson and taught it six times (three in the United States and three in Switzerland), rotating instructors and observers at each cycle. This meant one instructor and five observers per lesson. In addition, we (facilitators) also observed each lesson. We used our own high school science classrooms and those of selected colleagues. Selected colleagues would also observe the lesson and often offer feedback. Depending on our yearly goals for the group, some years teachers taught the lessons in Switzerland, other times in the United States and vice versa. After each lesson, the six teachers would debrief, with us present, and determine changes to be made prior to the next lesson enactment based on the data they had collected during the lesson. After the final LS debriefing session, the group members would together write a report detailing their experience at each cycle, including describing their individual and group learning. To better understand their thinking, ideas and learning during the experience, we also interviewed the teachers throughout their lesson study experience. Our goals for these collaborations were for these new teachers to increase their teaching effectiveness, particularly with diverse and marginalized pupils, and to develop greater cultural competence with pupils and colleagues.

## General guidelines for learner-centered facilitation

The foundations for learner-centered facilitation are setting group norms, using lesson study process guidelines, and developing and using reflective questions. At the outset of each project, our teachers have very little familiarity with LS. To develop their knowledge of LS and provide a common language for the group, we require teachers to read an article outlining the general process and purpose of LS that was specifically written for novices ("Action Research Through the Lens of Lesson Study", Lewis & Baker, 2010). Throughout the project, we continue to connect to the goals and process of LS as discussed in the article.

At our initial meeting, we begin by explicitly defining our role as facilitators. We communicate that we are there to guide the process and explain that the work and learning should happen within the group. We tell our teachers that we are like mirrors, reflecting what we see to them, and that we will use probing questions to sharpen the image. We let them know that we are not there to tell them what is right or wrong, or how to teach, but to help them develop a sense of effective practice so they can make their own decisions about good teaching. Finally, we outline group norms by stating several principles about the "space" of the LS group (see Figure 11.2). These norms include the need to use collaborative language, listening

---

*The lesson study group will be an equal and shared space*

1 All voices are valued and should be equally considered
2 Use collaborative language (i.e. "our" lesson rather "my" lesson)
3 Listen actively to learn, not to "win"
4 Focus on consensus, use compromise if necessary
5 All ideas are valid

---

*Figure 11.2* LS group norms

to learn rather than to win, finding consensus and keeping in mind that all voices are equal and valid. The norms are designed to give each teacher an equal voice and make the space of the LS group, whether while in a room together or in a video chat across the ocean, a place where teachers can take risks and learn from each other.

In addition to norms and the description of the facilitator role, our first meeting always includes an explanation of our overall goals and purpose. Our goals were that our teachers would increase their teaching effectiveness, especially related to marginalized pupils. To us this means that the groups would use a student-centered approach with attention to increasing relevancy to their students within their lessons.

Additionally, we provide the topic of the lesson and the group is expected to develop the specific learning objective. We learned to do this early on. For our second group (Group 2), we left the topic choice up to them. This group spent much of their lesson planning time debating a lesson topic, which left little time for discussing strategies to use or tasks to plan for learning.

Finally, in our initial meeting we give the teachers guidelines related to the process of LS (see Figure 11.3). We expect our teachers to purposefully use these guidelines to focus their planning.

In our case, the teachers live on two continents. This means that group meetings occur online using video chats or messaging until a travel exchange takes place. However, most of the work of the LS group occurs during the two week-long travel exchanges. During each exchange the teachers teach three lessons and meet several times daily. No matter the meeting format, the teachers are asked to appoint one group member to summarize decisions made and the reasoning for the decisions in an email to us. We use these summaries to help us understand the thinking, planning, and potential struggles of each group. Near the beginning of the ten-month project duration, the Swiss come to the United States for one week. During this time, three of the lessons are taught to three different classes. Near the end of the project, US group members go to Switzerland where the last three lessons are taught, again, to three different classes. The lessons are taught in our own classes, and additionally we ask selected public school teaching colleagues if they would allow our group one period to teach their lesson.

At least one of us attends whole group planning and debriefing meetings. Prior to the meeting, we meet and discuss what questions to pose based on group progress, struggles, and in relation to our goals for the teachers (i.e. increase teaching effectiveness especially for

---

*Guidelines for lesson study process*

1 Focus on the lesson, not on individual instructors
2 All teachers teach the lesson once
3 All teachers observe other lessons being taught and the group must create an observation data sheet considering at least pupil engagement (focus especially on marginalized pupils)
4 Teachers must collect data during the lesson on objective attainment by *all* pupils
5 Lesson should engage marginalized pupils, place-based planning should be considered to increase relevance
6 This is a learning opportunity, there is no wrong or right

*Figure 11.3* LS process guidelines

| |
|---|
| *Guidelines for facilitators during planning and debriefing meetings* |
| 1  Prior to meetings determine 2-4 foci for questioning based on desired learning outcomes for LS group<br>2  Listen<br>3  Ask reflective questions related to LS group objectives<br>4  Stay neutral, do not note what went well or is being done well, instead point teachers to research and data collected from lesson enactment (no judgement or advice)<br>   a  If teachers don't have needed data, questions focus on what data they will need from pupils to make a decision<br>5  When teachers directly ask for specific resources provide support<br>   a  For example – Our teachers used their data to determine that they were encountering student resistance to a lesson topic. They then asked for strategies to engage resistant students including those on ensuring relevance. We provided a resource on understanding student resistance, culturally relevant teaching practices, and ways to make lessons more meaningful (and relevant) to resistant students. |
| *Guidelines for facilitators during lesson enactment* |
| 1  Observe pupils. In our case for engagement due to LS group objective, particularly students who are traditionally marginalized in school (i.e. students who are emergent language learners, students with learning disabilities, students with autism, students of diverse ethnic or religious backgrounds, students who identify as LGBQT etc.)<br>2  Observe lesson strategies chosen by the group and how and if they are enacted in the way intended<br>3  Note questions to consider with co-facilitator and/or group<br>4  Videotape lesson enactment<br>5  Take pictures of pupil work/note visible pupil thinking from formative assessment<br>6  Do not interact with the LS group or the pupils |

*Figure 11.4* LS facilitator guidelines

marginalized pupils). During the meetings we listen, take notes and ask reflective questions (see Figure 11.4 and Case Spotlight 1).

At least one of us attends during lesson enactment. While five of the teachers observe and one instructs, we take detailed notes on pupil engagement, usually creating a map of the room and noting which students interact and how. We catalogue the tasks and strategies the group uses and note changes made between lessons. We also note if the intended strategies and tasks are implemented and how.

After each lesson is taught, we meet together and discuss trends seen in the lesson and determine questions to ask during the debriefing session related to these patterns and the LS group goals. We then sit in on the debriefing session and listen and ask the pre-determined reflective questions. We do not state whether the lesson went well or what was or was not effective in the lesson. We do ask questions that guide the group to think about these factors (see Case Spotlight 1). We guide the group to consider data they have related to student engagement and learning from their observations of the lesson as well as any pupil work. The whole group follows traditional Japanese LS debriefing guidelines (instructor speaks first, focus on the lesson not the instructor, use data from lesson observations to make points, etc.).

> **Case spotlight 1: reflective questions**
>
> Group 2 planned a teacher-centered PowerPoint lecture as the main learning opportunity in their first two lessons. Our observations and data collected during lessons showed a large percentage of pupils who were not engaged or meeting the objective, particularly students who were traditionally marginalized in schools.
>
> Our question foci related to the need for Group 2 to (1) increase student engagement and participation and (2) develop an assessment (and objective) of learning that went beyond surface-level questions. In our facilitator meetings, we concluded that if the group could focus on their lesson data they would be able to ascertain the need for particular lesson changes that would result in more student engagement and likely more learning.
>
> Reflective facilitator questions related to focus 1 (engagement):
>
> - What does your observational data on pupil engagement show?
> - How many different students answered questions? Which students?
> - When were students asking their own questions during the lesson?
> - What percent of the lesson was teacher talk? Student talk? What do you think is ideal and why?
> - What instructional strategies were used during the times students were and were not engaged?
>
> Reflective facilitator questions related to focus 2 (assessment):
>
> - What is your data related to how students are meeting your group's learning objective (e.g. that pupils will know the structure and function of DNA)?
> - How does this data tell you (or not) whether they have met the objective?
> - What other information might you need, and how could you get it?
> - How do you know students understand the function of DNA rather than just the structure? What is the evidence you have of their learning?

## Learner-centered facilitation in action

During each of our seven LS groups, we studied the teaching competencies of our six pre-service teachers. We found that at the end of the project they engaged in more student-centered thinking, including in their choice of lesson strategies (small-group discussions vs. whole-class lecture, inclusion of formative assessment, etc.), and were more able to navigate novel cultural settings (i.e. less likely to take something said by others as a personal attack). What we also found was that some of this shift in thinking was related to how the groups were facilitated rather than the process of LS itself. Pre-service teachers from Groups 1–7 said that they began to model their ideas about teaching based on the way we facilitated and on what they learned from the LS process.

An example illustrating this impact of learner-centered facilitation comes from our first group (Group 1). The teachers were genuinely surprised that we would not tell them what to do. Prior to teaching their first lesson, they "turned in the lesson plan" to us like an assignment, clearly expecting that we would tell them what was "good" or "bad". We told them that the format was correct and that their notes on what the teacher would do and the students would do were clear. We didn't evaluate, offer advice or judge their ideas or strategies. They all told us later that they were uncomfortable and surprised. At the time they asked us directly if it "was ok?" Our response was that they should pay close attention to the data they collect on student engagement and learning and that this will give them much of their answer. We asked them questions about the depth of the data they were collecting and what they might expect to learn from it. One group member said that she realized then we "were not going to tell them what to do" and that "we had to decide for ourselves . . . based on student data . . . whether something worked or not". She noted that this caused them all to re-examine their lesson and data collection methods. Each group member noted that this was "scary" because they "didn't want to screw up" and were sometimes unsure how to proceed. These same teachers also reported that this made them rely on each other more and to have more confidence in their approach because they felt they weren't being judged. It also caused them to carefully consider their methods, as they were responsible for pupil learning. The co-created group space became safe for exploring and learning.

In subsequent years, all other groups and many teachers from the groups noted that their teaching philosophy and approach was strongly impacted by how the LS group was facilitated, particularly that it was a space for them to reflect on their own thinking and where they had the freedom to learn from each lesson cycle without a fear of being judged. A learner-centered facilitation approach rests on trust that with well-crafted reflective questions, group norms and a process focused on participant learning, without evaluation, teachers will learn to better meet pupil needs (see Case Spotlight 2). We trusted our groups to learn from this process, even when they themselves did not.

### Case spotlight 2: learner-centered facilitation in action

Group 5 struggled to collaborate functionally as a whole group. Factions developed, fell, and then redeveloped in new ways. Some members felt they were doing more work. Other group members felt as though they were not heard and that only one or two voices were dominant due to several (potentially) cultural factors. We took several steps to support this group in a learner-centered way:

1  When they were frustrated, we had meetings with our respective teachers and listened and reflected back their ideas.
2  We regularly reiterated group norms and processes and asked group members to think of ways to put these into practice.

The teachers requested, in various ways, that we tell them what to do and solve the problems. We debriefed often to determine what the focus of our support and questions should be to these teachers who were truly struggling. We adhered to our learner-centered approach, trusting that if we told them how to proceed they would miss out on important learning opportunities in professionalism, collaborative experience and teaching effectiveness.

We eventually brought the conflict into the open with the group, asked them what the overall purpose of the project was (i.e. student learning and their effectiveness at promoting this based on evidence), and asked them questions relating to how to collaborate effectively and how this was related to group norms and processes. The group began to recognize that they needed to look within; we would not tell them how to proceed. We noticed then that group members started providing less self-centred responses and collaborating towards listening to learn rather than to win some point. It became more about what was best for their students' learning rather than being right about which strategy would work best. It became less personal and more professional.

This group ended with a collaboratively planned lesson using student-centered strategies. At the end, teachers said (some very enthusiastically) that it was difficult and frustrating, and at times they considered quitting. They also reported that they'd felt supported and "empowered" by our refusal to solve their issues and knew they had to choose their own ways to address their challenges. Some said it was the most powerful personal and professionally rewarding experience they'd ever had. All reported that in addition to developing a more in-depth understanding of how to meet diverse student needs, they also learned to "really collaborate". We still marvel at this group's growth and recognize that through sessions using pre-determined reflective questions, this group developed a more intrinsic understanding and adherence to the LS group norms and LS process. This learning enhanced what they were able to achieve by following the LS process.

## Learner-centered facilitation impact on future classroom practice

Many of the past participants in Groups 1–7 are current classroom teachers in the United States and Switzerland. We surveyed these teachers and asked them how they remembered our role as facilitators, what their most vivid memory of the LS experience was, and how the model of facilitation we used may have impacted their approach in their current classrooms.

These current teachers remembered distinctly our role as facilitators. Many discussed the neutral, non-evaluative attitude and safe group space, and also that what they carry into teaching from our learner-centered facilitation posture is the idea that people learn by constructing their understanding, and that this can be even more powerful when answers must be discovered through a collaborative, data-driven process. This is in contrast to passively being told how to do something or what the answers are, which describes the educational experiences of most of our teachers. Many recognized that this learner-centered disposition strongly and positively impacted their learning in the group, and they now use this approach with their students (see Table 11.1). Furthermore, their most vivid memories of the project centered around the times they were collaborating in the group; doing the work, discussing, thinking, and reflecting related to the LS goals (i.e. meeting the needs of marginalized pupils). One teacher, when asked his most vivid memory, sent a picture of the group of six standing around a table, leaning in towards each other, with papers and proposed lesson materials spread all around. Each participant was openly smiling and engaged.

One impact that the teachers repeatedly described is related to the professional development impacts of using LS in general and the overall goals we selected for the project. However, these impacts seem to be bolstered by the facilitation approach. Teachers said that they actively seek ways to understand the engagement and learning of all of their students (some of them italicized or boldfaced the word "all"). These teachers try to diversify their teaching

Table 11.1 Themes related to the role of facilitators

| Themes across teachers remembering the role of their LS facilitator | Teachers' most vivid memory | Teachers' perceived impact of learner-centered facilitation on their current teaching |
|---|---|---|
| • Guiding for learning rather than telling<br>• The importance of struggle in learning process<br>• Promoting thinking process<br>• Foster focus on learning outcomes<br>• Give everybody a voice<br>• Provide support and understanding<br>• No judgement/neutral stance<br>• Allow time and space to find specific group solutions to barriers | • Collaboration<br>• Reflection time<br>• Group discussion | • Desire to diversify teaching style<br>• Recognize the power of language in the science classroom<br>• Use pupil observation for instructional information<br>• Seeking ways to help learner understand<br>• Seeking ways to assess engagement and learning<br>• Question myself<br>• Teacher metacognition, reflexivity |

strategies to reach all learners, to pay attention to the engagement of their pupils and to choose assessment strategies that allow them to understand student learning and thinking in relation to their objectives. They said that this seemed to be a direct result of the facilitation style, which helped them develop a process for analyzing student learning. This outcome is also likely related to using an LS approach in general.

When considering the long-term effects of learner-centered facilitation, many of the teachers referred to the impact of our neutral/non-judgemental stance. Particularly important seems to be that we helped them develop a safe space for collaborative planning and using student data to determine teaching effectiveness without offering our evaluation. Some of these teachers seem to see this as room to "make mistakes" and that the guidance within this space, perhaps through reflective questions, supported their learning. Several teachers decided to take this approach in their classroom, seeking to allow their pupils space and time to struggle, to grapple, to come to their own conclusions or to dive into their own inquiries. In this space they assume a neutral stance, one that reflects back the ideas and thoughts of their students, using questions to guide thinking. The thoughts and actions of these teachers helped us to understand how our style is impactful on groups – a neutral, non-judgemental stance, allowing learning through cause and effect ("making mistakes"), asking groups to think for themselves and "solve their own problems" and guiding rather than telling. It seems that learner-centered facilitation offers a way to lead LS groups in a manner that has an impact beyond the original LS experience; it is a way that teachers select as an approach for facilitating student learning in their own classroom.

## Conclusions and recommendations

Using a learner-centered facilitative approach for lesson study is a way to increase the effectiveness of the LS process. Group members inherently grapple with ideas and struggle productively with the tasks embedded in LS. However, when paired with a focus on group norms, deliberately planned reflective questions, and a non-evaluative stance, it enhances the learning of LS group members. Not only do they learn and apply the process of using student generated evidence to make instructional decisions in a collaborative space, but they also can develop a way to more independently determine lesson effectiveness and interact with their own students. In this manner the facilitation process becomes itself a learning opportunity for teachers. This type of facilitation models an effective approach for developing lesson tasks, one that teachers can use as facilitators in their own classrooms. Using this approach, however, the facilitator must be able to let go of the idea that their expertise must drive the process and trust the group and the process of constructing understanding. To do this, facilitators must believe that learning will occur when teachers struggle, collaborate and follow the process. Being thoughtful about how the teachers are learning, taking time before responding to participant questions, and planning for and using reflective questions rather than suggestions, tips or advice about how to proceed are all methods of maintaining a learner-centered facilitation approach. Additionally, co-facilitating is a way we have found that assures continuation of this kind of approach. We have spent hours collaboratively developing reflective questions for groups. However, we also cannot count the number of times we have given each other a "look" or a nudge under the table that says to the other, "stop talking and telling, they've got this".

## Additional readings

Azevedo, R., Behnagh, R., Duffy, M., Harley, J., & Trevors, G. (2012). Metacognition and self-regulated learning in student-centered learning environments. In *Theoretical foundations of student-centered learning environments* (pp. 171–197). New York, NY: Routledge.

Bartolini, M. G., & Ramploud, A. (2018). Il Lesson Study per la formazione degli insegnanti. Carocci Faber ed. 211 pp.

Brand, B. R., & Moore, S. J. (2011). Enhancing teachers' application of inquiry-based strategies using a constructivist sociocultural professional development model. *International Journal of Science Education*, *33*(7), 889–913. https://doi.org/10.1080/09500691003739374

Cajkler, W., & Wood, P. (2016). Mentors and student-teachers "lesson-studying" in initial teacher education. *International Journal for Lesson and Learning Studies*, *5*(2), 84–98.

De Vries, S., Prenger, R., & Poortman, C. (2017). A lesson study professional learning network in secondary education. Conference paper presented at *ICSEI*, Ottawa.

Hiebert, J., Morris, A. K., Berk, D., & Jansen, A. (2007). Preparing teachers to learn from teaching. *Journal of Teacher Education*, *58*(1), 47–61.

Johnson, J., Perez, L., & Uline, C. (2013). *Teaching practices from America's best urban schools*. New York, NY: Routledge.

Lewis, C., & Baker. (2010). Action research through the lens of lesson study. In R. Pelton (Ed.), *Action research for teacher candidates: Using classroom data to enhance instruction*. UK: Rowman and Littlefield Education.

Lutovac, S., Kaasila, R., & Juuso, H. (2015). Video-stimulated recall as a facilitator of a pre-service teacher's reflection on teaching and post-teaching supervision discussion: A case study from Finland. *Journal of Education and Learning*, *4*(3), 14–24.

Richardson, V. (1998). How teachers change. *Focus on Basics*, *2*(C).

# 12 Conclusion

## How do we judge the success of lesson study adaptations?

*Catherine Lewis*

The chapters of this volume attest to the widespread interest in lesson study and the thoughtful work of educators around the world. In the two decades since the first English language lesson study publications appeared (Lewis & Tsuchida, 1998; Stigler & Hiebert, 1999), lesson study has spread to diverse regions of the world and educators have developed tools and adaptations that can advance lesson study practice locally and perhaps more broadly. How can we judge which of these tools and adaptations would be useful in our own settings?

Back in 2002, I likened lesson study to sushi; they are both quintessentially Japanese traditions that have gained surprisingly large followings in North America (Lewis, 2002). A program officer at the US National Science Foundation pursued this comparison by asking me whether the sushi and lesson study created by Americans were palatable – or even recognizable – to Japanese. With respect to sushi, we know the answer. Some North American inventions, such as the avocado-crab "California Roll," have been widely reverse-imported to Japan, delighting Japanese sushi lovers, who pay top dollar for this US innovation! What about the adaptations of lesson study around the world? Are educators making important lesson study modifications that will build its effectiveness in diverse regions, perhaps even contributing to Japanese practice? In other words, are we making a lesson study analogue of the delectable California Roll? Or are we creating something closer to the Peanut Butter Sushi my 10-year-old son once concocted with a friend? (It was good for developing my son's culinary identity and cooking skills, but perhaps not widely appealing to others.) How can we gauge the usefulness of adaptations that are arising around the world? Are they California Rolls or Peanut Butter Sushi?

Figure 12.1 provides a framework for considering the contributions of this volume. Visible above the water are the lesson study features the chapters discuss, some of which (like *kyouzai kenkyuu*) originated in Japan, and others of which (like learner-centred facilitation) originated outside Japan. Underneath the water are the currents of growth that make lesson study effective: currents of growth in educators' knowledge, beliefs, practice, agency and collegial social capital (collegial trust and communication). I separate the visible features of lesson study from the underlying changes because educators are too often told to focus on visible features without sufficient attention to the underlying goals of the work. The underlying goals of lesson study are to nurture productive changes in teachers' knowledge, beliefs, practice, agency and collegial capital.

The chapters of this volume provide some evidence about how the visible features might stimulate these important currents of growth. For example, *kyouzai kenkyuu* builds teachers' knowledge of curriculum and content, mock-up lessons build enactment of knowledge in practice and open-ended tasks build teachers' knowledge of student thinking. Some features discussed in the chapters are likely to support change in more than one area; for example,

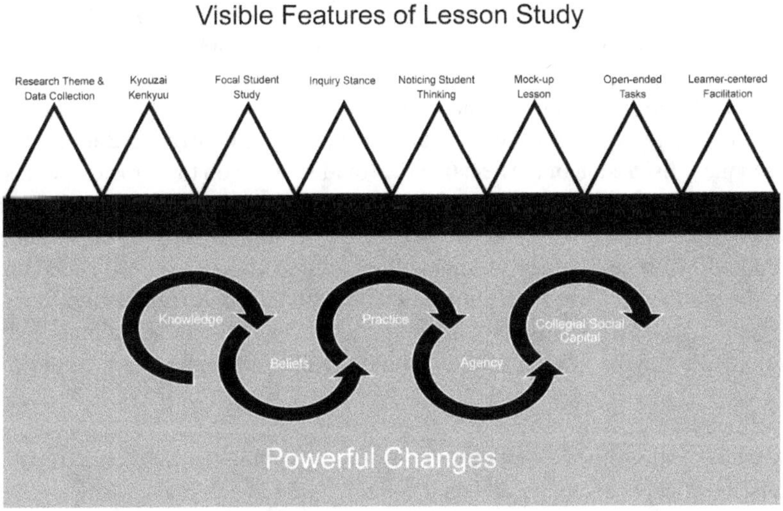

## Visible Features of Lesson Study

*Figure 12.1* Visible features and underlying changes of lesson study

successful learner-centred facilitation should support teachers' knowledge development, sense of agency, student-centred beliefs about effective teaching and collegial social capital.

Figure 12.1 helps us think about three points related to effective lesson study. First, the visible features do not have a simple relationship to the underlying currents of growth. The model is not made of arrows and mechanical parts but of natural features – an environment in which the interaction of many geographical features shapes currents of growth. Establishing the features shown in the upper half does not automatically create the currents of change shown at the bottom, since the overall underwater geography shapes the currents. However, the mountains do serve as helpful signposts; if *kyouzai kenkyuu* is happening, teachers are likely to be building knowledge (unless the work is undermined by some other feature of the environment, such as poor materials chosen for study or a top-down, compliance-focused approach that undermines teachers' learning). To summarize, focusing on the visible features of lesson study, while important, does not tell us whether the powerful changes are occurring.

Figure 12.1 also helps us think about developmental changes in lesson study over time. Lesson study groups change over time, like the natural environment. Features that produced currents of growth at one point in a group's history may not do so several years later. Protocols may come to feel superfluous, or outdated, or confining. Seasoned lesson study practitioners may need something quite different from first-year teams. One goal of facilitation in a brand-new lesson study group may be to render facilitation obsolete over time, by creating a seasoned team that has internalized the processes and values of learner-centred facilitation.

Figure 12.1 also highlights the idea that multiple currents of growth are needed for powerful changes, and that these currents affect each other. The swirling of one current affects the others in ways that may not be easy to predict. If any one of the currents is neglected for too long, lesson study is unlikely to be effective or sustained. For example, if lesson study builds teachers' knowledge but not their agency to act on knowledge, or if lesson study helps teachers build productive beliefs about good instruction but not the capacity to enact their beliefs in practice, teachers will not find lesson study useful and will not sustain it. To make matters even more complicated, the different currents of growth often compete for attention – for example, when a facilitator must decide whether to support teachers' agency as inquirers or simply give them high-quality content resources. Morago and Grigioni Baur highlight such trade-offs in their discussion of the decision to provide the lesson topic to novice lesson study teams rather than have groups spend time finding a topic. One could imagine this is precisely the right decision in their setting (pre-service teachers) but that for more experienced teachers, the trade-off between agency (allowing the group to choose its topic) and competence (ensuring the group will learn something valuable from the cycle) might be different.

As we reflect on our lesson study work and consider whether to adopt practices featured in this volume, it may be helpful to think about the following questions, in the context of Figure 12.1:

1. How well is lesson study supporting our team's growth in the five domains: knowledge, beliefs, practice, agency and collegial capital? Is there a domain where we would like to strengthen our growth? Consider asking all team members to reflect briefly in writing about how lesson study has contributed to their growth in each of those domains, share responses as willing and use the team's reflections to guide future work.
2. What new features (perhaps drawn from this volume) might help us support growth in the particular current(s) of growth we would like to strengthen? For example, what features might help our team build knowledge, agency and so forth? What might be the impact of the new features on the *other* currents of growth? Might the new feature adversely affect growth in one of the other domains? For example, when designing a randomized trial of fractions lesson study that included project-supplied fractions resources in a lesson study resource kit, I worried that the project-supplied fractions resources would undermine teachers' sense of agency. That did not turn out to be the case in that study (Lewis & Perry, 2015, 2017), which showed positive impact on student learning, teacher learning and teacher beliefs about the efficacy of collegial work, but it seems to be the case in our later work that is still unfolding.

Where do the "powerful changes" at the base of Figure 12.1 come from? Four decades of research based in self-determination theory (Deci & Ryan, 1985; Ryan & Deci, 2000, 2017) suggests that human beings develop intrinsic motivation in settings that meet their basic human needs for agency,[1] belonging and competence. (Some teachers have dubbed these human needs "the new ABCs".) We human beings are intrinsically motivated to work hard in settings that support our agency, that give us a sense of belonging to a valued group and that help us develop competence at tasks we value (Solomon, Battistich, Watson, Schaps, & Lewis, 2000). The five currents of growth shown at the bottom of Figure 12.1 are based on self-determination theory, with the "competence" dimension elaborated into three currents (knowledge, beliefs, practice) in order to capture the complexity of competence in teaching, which includes development of many kinds of knowledge, productive beliefs about students and the capacity to enact these in practice.

Self-determination theory also implies that the powerful changes at the bottom of Figure 12.1 will support lesson study sustainability because we human beings are also motivated to internalize the values of settings that meet our needs for agency, belonging and competence (Battistich, Solomon, Kim, Watson, & Schaps, 1995). Human beings maintain and value

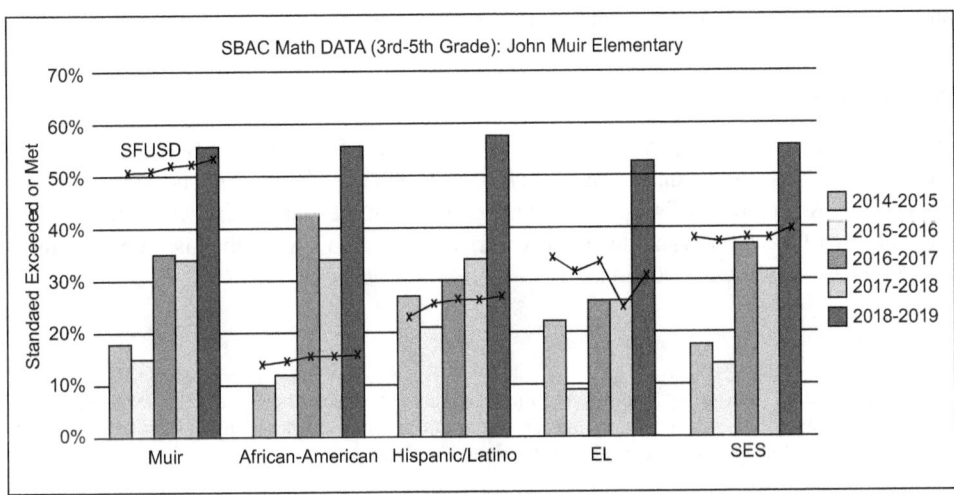

*Figure 12.2* Mathematics SBAC, John Muir Elementary School (San Francisco)

groups that help us develop competence, agency and collegial relationships. Teacher-led, self-sustained, school-wide lesson study has emerged in several schools in the San Francisco–Oakland area of California, and review of online video of their pre-lesson and post-lesson discussions provides a rich resource for considering the nature of sustainable lesson study, fuelled by teachers' agency, competence and colleagueship. (Video is available at www.lessonresearch.net, under resources for school-wide lesson study.)

As you peruse the resources on school-wide lesson study, consider Figure 12.2, which highlights what teacher-led, school-wide lesson study has been able to accomplish in some schools. The data in Figure 12.2 come from a San Francisco elementary school that serves predominantly low-income students, including 30% of families who experience housing insecurity. Figure 12.2 shows the growth in SBAC (the state standardized mathematics assessment) from 2014 (left-most column in each group) to 2019 (right-most column) for each of the major subgroups at the school. ("SES" designates low income.) The scores for the district as a whole (which serves a much higher-income, White, native-English population than the school) are shown by the line of x's. The school began to build school-wide lesson study, focused on mathematics, during the 2015–2016 school year, starting with a few teams and building school-wide over the next three years. Their *kyouzai kenkyuu* has drawn heavily on Japanese Teaching Through Problem-Solving and on mathematical reasoning interviews developed by Math Solutions. Teacher leadership (built through a district-supported network of teacher fellows) has been a hallmark of the work.

If the chapters of this book and the work of teachers involved in school-wide lesson study has whet your appetite to step up your own lesson study work, you can find an extensive set of tools in the Conduct-a-Cycle section of the website www.lessonresearch.net organized around each phase of the lesson study cycle.

Lesson study is not a static or rigid process but one that, in Japan and around the world, is constantly evolving to address a diverse and changing educational environment. Equipped with the many interesting ideas highlighted in this book, the opportunities for further learning at sites like www.lessonresearch.net and the reflection questions that help us connect lesson study features to underlying currents of learning, I wish us all productive next steps in our lesson study journeys. I hope we can share reactions and updates in future meetings, virtual and in person, of the World Association of Lesson Studies.

## Acknowledgements

Work described in this chapter was funded by the Institute for Education Sciences of the US Department of Education under Grant No. R305A150043 and by the Bill and Melinda Gates Foundation. Any opinions, findings, conclusions, or recommendations expressed in this chapter are those of the authors and do not necessarily reflect the views of the Institute for Education Sciences or of the Foundation.

## Note

1 Originally called "autonomy" but often termed "agency" by educators to avoid the seeming contradiction between autonomy and belonging. The autonomy/agency construct emphasizes freedom from aversive control and a feeling of authorship of one's actions.

## Additional readings

Battistich, V., Solomon, D., Kim, D., Watson, M., & Schaps, E. (1995). Schools as communities, poverty levels of student populations, and students' attitudes, motives, and performance: A multilevel analysis. *American Educational Research Journal*. https://doi.org/10.3102%2F00028312032003627

Deci, E., & Ryan, R. (1985). *Intrinsic motivation and self-determination in human behavior*. New York, NY: Plenum.

Lewis, C. (2002). Does lesson study have a future in the United States? *Nagoya Journal of Education and Human Development*, *1*(1), 1–23.

Lewis, C., & Perry, R. (2015). A randomized trial of lesson study with mathematical resource kits: Analysis of impact on teachers' beliefs and learning community. In E. J. Cai & J. Middleton (Eds.), *Design, results, and implications of large-scale studies in mathematics education* (pp. 133–155). Springer.

Lewis, C., & Perry, R. (2017). Lesson study to scale up research-based knowledge: A randomized, controlled trial of fractions learning. *Journal for Research in Mathematics Education*, *48*(3), 261. https://doi.org/10.5951/jresematheduc.48.3.0261

Lewis, C., & Tsuchida, I. (1998, Winter). A lesson is like a swiftly flowing river: Research lessons and the improvement of Japanese education. *American Educator*, *22*, 14–17, 50–52.

Ryan, R. M., & Deci, E. L. (2017). *Self-determination theory: Basic psychological needs in motivation, development, and wellness*. New York, NY: Guilford Press.

Ryan, R. M., & Deci, E. L. (2000). Self-determination theory and the facilitation of intrinsic motivation, social development, and well-being. *American Psychologist*, *55*(1), 68.

Solomon, D., Battistich, V., Watson, M., Schaps, E., & Lewis, C. (2000). A six-district study of educational change: Direct and mediated effects of the child development project. *Social Psychology of Education*, *4*, 3–51.

Stigler, J. W., & Hiebert, J. (1999). *The teaching gap: Best ideas from the world's teachers for improving education in the classroom*. New York, NY: Free Press.

www.lessonresearch.net provides an extensive introduction to lesson study, video, tools and examples from each phase of the lesson study cycle, and cases from school-wide lesson study sites that have used mathematics Teaching Through Problem-Solving.

# Index

Note: Page numbers in *italic* indicate a figure and page numbers in **bold** indicate a table on the corresponding page.

actionable artefacts 50
active involvement 66
adults, and seeing 16
area and perimeter (mathematics), lesson study on 4–6
area model 61
assumptions, making 100–101

Begin With One Number (BWON) strategies 29, 30, 37–38
blind spots, teachers' 48
blockades 97
board plan *62, 63*
Bocala, C. 73
body balance 79
Bohm, D. 97
bulletin board problem 7
BWON strategy *see* Begin With One Number (BWON) strategies

California Academy of Sciences 44
Cambridge Oracy Assessment Toolkit 70
case pupils 14, 15, 18, 25; role of *17*
Cervetti, G. 69
Choy B. H. 2, 44, 46
classrooms 76; as research labs 13
classroom knowledge 67
classroom research 94
Clerc-Georgy, A. 2
Clivaz, S. 2
co-curriculum designers 45
cognitive area, the 70
collaborative learners 17
collaborative professionals, teachers as 17, 50
collegial relationships 119
collegial social capital 117
Common Core State Standards for Mathematics 53, 59
communication: conversations as subject of 98; in teaching 79

communications problems 98
competence 67
conception of quantities **37**
Conduct-a-Cycle section 119
consensus-seeking behaviours 71
conversational moves, facilitator role modelling through 103–104
conversations, protocols for 69–71
Conway, P. 67
core mathematics 61
critical reflective dialogue *102*
cross-cultural pre-service teachers 106, 107
curriculum guides/materials 44–45, 49
curriculum study phase 2

Decompose Tens and Ones (DTO) strategy 29, 33–34, 37
deficit thinking 103
Department of the Professional Development of Teachers (DPDT) 45
devil's advocate 72
De Vries, S. 2
Dewey, J. 71
Doyle, W. 67
DTO strategy *see* Decompose Tens and Ones (DTO) strategy
Dudley, P. 1, 2, 18

*Elementary School Guide to Examining Content and Unit Planning* 63; excerpt from *64*
English as a foreign language (EFL) 76; and lesson study (LS) cycle 81–84
English classrooms, lesson study in 16–17
equivalent fractions 58–64, *59*–61
Eraut, M. 67
evidence-based knowledge 67
expert practice, and noticing 76
exploratory conversations *98*
exploratory talk 17, 25, 95, 100; modelling 103, *103*; vs qualifying and cumulative talk 98–99

Fabrega, J. 2
facilitators 2; as convenor 86–87; detection of group resistance 99; and developing inquiry stance 97–99; as group members 90–91; guidelines *110*; as knowledgeable others 92; lessons learned 92; as researchers 89–90; role of **114**; roles of 104–105, 109; and suggestions for guiding teachers *105*; as teacher trainers 88–89; training 91–92
formal knowledge 73
Friedkin, S. 2
future classroom practice 113–114

goal system interview *101*
Grigioni Baur, S. 2, 118
Grimen, H. 67
ground rules 17; for teacher-talk 25
group, knowledge development in 73, 117
group protocol, questions for *98*
guiding questions 46–47

Helgevold, N. 2
heroes 28
high-leverage mathematical ideas 58
*Houghton Mifflin Harcourt Math Curriculum* 60

individual thought, and language 66
individual utterances *96*
inquiry stance 94; challenges adopting 96–97; characteristics of *94*; creating safe environment for 99; roles to develop 97–99
instructional decisions, using students' mistakes 27–28
instructional materials 39; redesigning 49; research 40
inter-thinking 17
International Bureau of Education at UNESCO 44

Jackson, W. C. 42
Japan 39; knowledgeable others in 45; lesson study practice in 45; and teacher professional effort 1
Japanese math textbooks 44–45
*jugyo kenkyuu* 7

know how/ knowing how 66, 67
knowing about 73
knowing that 67
knowledge, role of in teaching 66–68
knowledgeable others 45, 48–49, 50; external 49
knowledge development 66, 71
knowledge resources /sources 2, 67; and systematic data collection 73–74; and teachers' conversations 72–74; and theories and research 72–73
Kvam, E. K. 2
*kyouzai kenkyuu* 2, 39–40; challenges in 49–50; and effective lesson study 50; improving 42–44; and primary science teachers 41; record sheet 77–78, **79**, 85; record sheet, after practicum 80; record sheet, before practicum 78–79; record sheet, during practicum 80; in a Singapore classroom 46–49; and teachers' knowledge 116; what it is 39–40; worksheet, questions in

Lang, J. 1, 2, 18
language 73; barriers, and learning 79; for the group 108; and individual thought 66
Larssen, D. S. 2
Lausanne Laboratory Lesson Study (3LS) 86
Lausanne University of Teacher Education (HEP Vaud) 86
learner-centered facilitation 2–3, 106–107, *107*, 111–113; background 107–108; and future classroom practice 113–114; general 108–110; guidelines 108–109; long-term effect of 114; and teachers' knowledge development 117
learning goals, operationalizing 58
learning vocabulary 68–69, 72, 73
Lee, K.E.C. 2
lesson debrief 6, 108
lesson goals, goals 4
lessons, planning 67
lesson study (LS) 1; on area and perimeter (mathematics) 4–6; debriefing stage of 6, 27, 108; developmental changes in 117; and English classrooms 16–17; facilitation of 2; forms 74; global reach of 116; judging success of 116–120; and *kyouzai kenkyuu* 50; and learner-centered facilitation 114–115; nature of 97–98; process guidelines *109*; purpose of 100; as research 7–12; school-wide 119; stages of 18–24; sustainable 119; teacher-led 119; and understanding mistakes 35–36; visible features of *117*
lesson study (LS) facilitators 86, 106
lesson study conversations 2
lesson study cycle 17, 27, 63, 73; creating a safe climate for 97–99; in EFL 81–84; findings from 63; goals 13; group norms *108*; inquiry stance in 94; knowledgeable others and 45; the process of 100–104; value of mock-up lesson to 64
lesson study groups 2, 18, 106; comparison of 73–74; and language 66
lesson study practice: in Japan 45; outside of Japan 49
lesson study process *17*
lesson study reports 25
lesson study team 52, 58; conversations in 95–96; and mathematics learning 27

manipulatives *30*; use of 33–34
math coaches (MC) 60, 63
mathematical activity, inclusive 28–29

mathematical strategies/thinking 34, 45
mathematics: 86; methods of learning 14–17
mathematics learning: concepts in 16; and
    student's mistakes 32
mathematics lesson 27
Mathematics SBAC *119*
*Math Expressions* 59–60
Math Solutions 119
McDougal, T. 92
Ministry of Education's (MOE) primary science
    syllabus 41; framework 42
mock-up lesson 2, 52–53, *53*, 58; board plan
    after *63*; board plan during 62; knowledgeable
    others and 60
Morago, S. 2, 118
multi-digit operations/subtraction lesson
    28, 37
Munthe, E. 2, 67
Murata, A, 1
mutual trust 2, 97

Naesheim-Bjørkvik, G. 2
National Council of Teachers of Mathematics
    (NCTM) 44
National Science Teachers Association (NSTA) 44
Nemeth, C. 72
neutral/non-judgemental stance 114
non-verbal and paraverbal communication 79
Northern California 108
Notice/noticing 76, 85; developmental trajectory
    of 76; learning to 16
novice teachers 25, 107, 108
number bonds/relationships 33, 37

open-ended activity 27, 29, *35*
open-ended assessment 7
open-ended lesson activities 2
open-ended problems 7
open-ended tasks 29, 116
oracy framework: cognitive area, the 70; social
    and emotional 70–71
Organisation for Economic Co-operation and
    Development (OECD) 44

PDCA-cycle 98
pedagogical approaches 79
pedagogical practices: challenging 68–69;
    conversations about 71; exploring 68–69
physical education (PE) 76
place-value concept 37
post-lesson pupil interviews 16
post research lesson 14, 17, 21; lesson 2
    discussion 14; lesson 3 discussion *15, 16*
practical knowledge 66, 94
*practical syntheses* 67, 68
practical work, theories and 73
practicum: EFL, before 81–82; EFL, during
    83–84; *kyouzai kenkyuu*, after practicum

80; *kyouzai kenkyuu*, during practicum 80;
    *kyouzai kenkyuu* record sheet before 78–79
pre-service education 2
pre-service teachers 4, 108, 111; cross-cultural
    106, 107; and *kyouzai kenkyuu* 77–79; and
    lesson study 84–85; and lesson study (LS)
    76–77; observation research assignment
    81–84
primary science teachers, and *kyouzai kenkyuu* 41
prior knowledge, students 58
problem-solving approach, structured 45
problem-solving lesson 63; developing a 58–64
problem-solving tasks, engaging students in
    59–61; unit 59
professional development, of pre-service
    teachers 76
professional expertise 16
professional learning: cycles 67; and teachers 66
professional practice 67
prompts, use of 80, 85
propositional knowledge 67
pupil interviews 14, 17, 21–22, 25; post-lesson 16

quiet students 29

real-life students 18–24; post lesson discussion
    and 22–24; post lesson discussion record *23*;
    sequenced research lessons and 24; thinking
    point 2 *18*; thinking point 4 *22*
rectangles *5*
reflection and consolidation *104*; stimulating 104
reflective facilitator questions 111–112
rehearsal opportunity 53
researchers' stance 13
research lesson instructor 52
research lessons: plan *60*; sequenced 24, 25
Research Lesson Study (RLS) 15
research points, examples of *7*
research questions *102*; formulating 100
research skills 100
resistance, dealing with 99
Ricks, T. E. 44
run, calculating *47*
Ryle, G. 66

safe space, for collaborative planning 114
San Francisco Bay area 52
San Francisco elementary school 119
scaffolding tools 76–85
Schoenfeld, Alan, Teaching for Robust
    Understanding Project 30
School B *16*
School C *15*
schools, and teacher education institutes 49–50
science classrooms 108
science teachers, primary, and *kyouzai kenkyuu* 41
scientific knowledge 67, 72–73
self-determination theory 118

self-reliance, team's 104
sequenced research lessons 24, 25
shared knowledge, production of 66
Shimizu, Y. 40
Shulman, L. S. 67
Singapore 41, 44; *kyouzai kenkyuu* in a classroom 46–49
Smithsonian 44
social justice, mathematics for 28
social situation, using talk in 70
sociocultural theory 66
strategic knowledge 67
structured problem-solving approach 45
student-centred beliefs 117
student-centred teaching practices 1
students, assessing understanding of 58
students' mistakes 34; analyzing 2; and instructional implications 32, 34–35; and mathematics problems 32
student solutions 61
study lesson facilitators, and developing inquiry stance 97–99
subtraction problem 37
Switzerland 86, 107, 108
systematic data collection, knowledge resources 73–74

Takahashi, A. 92
talk 66; quality of talk 71
task 68–69, *72*, 73
teacher conversations 66, 74–75
teacher demographic data **28**
teacher educators 106
teacher leadership 119
teacher learning: collaborative 17; debriefing session and 29–31
teacher noticing 2
teacher professional development 1
teacher-pupil interaction 79
teachers 71; as collaborative professionals 50; conversations between 66, 69–71; and inquiry stance 94; and lesson study cycles 66; and professional learning 66

teachers' conversations: improving 69–71; knowledge resources and 72–74
teacher-talk, ground rules for 25
teacher trainers 88–89
teaching, role of knowledge in 66–68
*Teaching and Learning Guides* 44
Teaching for Robust Understanding Project (Schoenfeld) 30
Teaching Through Problem-Solving (TTP) lesson 60, 119; phases of 59
teams, resistance from 99; and self-reliance 104
textbooks/instructional materials 40
theoretical knowledge 73
theory and practice, connecting *96*
thinking box 2 *33*
thinking point 2 *18*
three-point framework 44, 46
Tokyo Shoseki's *Mathematics International* 44, 45
training facilitators 91–92
trust, mutual 97

Uffen, I. 2
United States 44
unit on "light" **41**
University of Stavanger, Norway (UiS) 76
US National Science Foundation 116

Van Es, E. A. 76
vocabulary learning. *See* learning vocabulary
volume, understanding of 53–58

Watanabe, T. 40
whole-class environment 76
worksheet, questions in *47*
World Association of Lesson Studies 120
Wright, T. S. 69

Xu, H. 18

Yang, Y. 44
Yoshida, M. 42, 44

For Product Safety Concerns and Information please contact our EU
representative  GPSR@taylorandfrancis.com
Taylor & Francis Verlag GmbH, Kaufingerstraße 24, 80331 München, Germany

www.ingramcontent.com/pod-product-compliance
Lightning Source LLC
Chambersburg PA
CBHW060514300426
44112CB00017B/2670